Please return or renew this item before the latest date shown

Renewals can be made
by internet   www.fifedirect.org.uk/libraries
in person   at any library in Fife
by phone   08451 55 00 66

Fife
COUNCIL

Thank you for using your library

ADLARD COLES NAUTICAL
LONDON

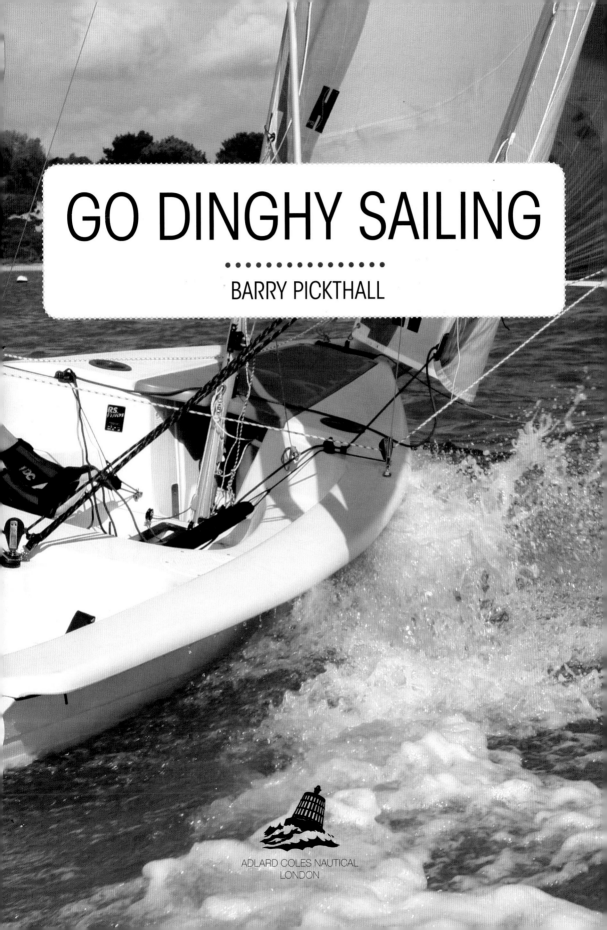

GO DINGHY SAILING

BARRY PICKTHALL

ADLARD COLES NAUTICAL
LONDON

CONTENTS

INTRODUCTION

Sailing a dinghy is one of the most exhilarating experiences. There is nothing more satisfying than harnessing the wind for free, to skim at speed across the water with the boat in perfect balance, or defying logic by sailing into the wind with great efficiency. It is a sport that, once smitten with, you never tire of. It's a participatory pastime that gets you out into the fresh air, keeps you fit, and tests the mind – and you can do it cheaply from the age of 5 to 85 or older.

You can potter about on a river, lake or sea, or join a club and graduate to racing around the buoys. And then who knows, you or your children could be inspired to follow Olympic multi-medallist Ben Ainslie to the top levels of the sport. With sailing, there really is no limit to aspirations or to the fun of getting afloat.

This book aims to inspire novices of all ages to give sailing a try. It prepares the reader for each stage, from where to sail to providing advice on the types of boat available. It takes you step-by-step through the basics of sailing and getting out on the water safely. If you know someone more experienced to take you out on the water for a first taster, then so much the better, but if not, there are clubs and sailing schools across the country where you will be welcomed with open arms.

Sailing is like that. It is a social sport that welcomes newcomers, so come on in, get your feet wet, and give it a try!

Barry Pickthall

1.GETTING STARTED

Look at any open stretch of water, and you will find a boat. And if it is a popular spot, there will almost certainly be a sailing club and slipway to launch from too. Sailing is a great participatory pastime, with as many people going afloat each weekend as there are attending football matches.

You will find sailing enthusiasts enjoying their sport on man-made gravel pits, lakes, reservoirs, rivers and all around the coast. It has become a favourite activity for the disabled too, sailing boats either designed or adapted for the purpose.

Learning to sail in a general-purpose dinghy is the easiest way to start. They are both light and simple, and easy to prepare. They are also very responsive, so any adjustment or movement within the boat has an immediate effect. Boats like the Wayfarer, Laser Bahia and RS Vision are good stable family boats, but you learn the ropes just as easily on a singlehander like the Laser, Optimist, Topper or Pico, especially if there is someone on-hand to coach you.

The best way to learn is to enrol with a registered sailing school. They will run courses for juniors, seniors and family groups, and having taken you through a structured curriculum, you will come away with a certificate of competence. If you are looking for a less formal introduction and don't know anyone to take you afloat, then you will be welcomed with open arms at any local sailing club where members are always short of crew. Many clubs also run training sessions themselves, especially for children, and host fun, introductory sailing courses during the school holidays to give youngsters a first taste.

2. WHERE TO SAIL?

A BASE TO SAIL FROM

So where do I start?

For many, first base is a local sailing club. Go along as a visitor, introduce yourself and ask if they run a course for beginners or if anyone needs a crew. If you live near a sailing area, visit several clubs and then make a judgement on which one best meets your needs.

You can then look at the various classes each club supports and get some experience in them. Then you will be better placed to decide which type of boat is for you. Avoid the temptation of buying a boat on a whim. You will invariably finish up with a dud; one that is out-dated, unsuited and one that will most probably put you off sailing for life. Far better to buy a class of boat already adopted by a club where members are on hand to help, advise and encourage you.

There are other fun ways to learn. Charter companies like Sunsail and Mark Warner offer package holidays in warm sun-drenched sailing centres around the world with sailing lessons included. Just as simply, you can enrol at any sailing school and learn the ropes during an intensive week of tuition, to give you the confidence and skills to take a boat out on your own.

Getting started is as simple as that!

3. CHOOSING A BOAT

CHOOSING THE RIGHT TYPE OF BOAT

The strong advice is to learn the basics at a sailing school or club before buying a boat. Once you know the ropes, you will have a much better idea about the type that will best suit your needs.

If you plan to join a club, then select one of the classes they have adopted and you will find plenty of advice and help on hand. If you simply want a boat to mess about in, then choose one that is light enough to launch and recover easily.

Trapeze-rigged dinghies offer higher performance but require greater experience to sail them. Starting out in a singlehander provides the fastest route to learning to sail, but if this is to be a family affair, there are plenty of general-purpose dinghies to choose from.

If stability is an issue, then a keelboat provides dinghy-like performance without the possibility of capsizing. These have a weighted keel instead of a centreboard, and with some, this can be raised to simplify launching, recovery and storage. They may also have winches which make it easier to handle what are often larger sails than on a dinghy.

● JUNIOR PRIMERS

Optimist

This box-like boat, first designed in 1947, has become a universal primer with large fleets in every corner of the globe amounting to some 130,000 registered worldwide. It was designed for home-competition from two sheets of plywood, but the majority are now moulded. It has a simple gaff rig, and the boat is light and small enough for one person to lift it up and off a car roof rack.

Length:	7.75ft	2.36m
Beam:	3.75ft	1.12m
Mainsail:	25sq.ft	3.3sq.m
Mast:	7.5ft	2.26m
Weight:	275lb	125kg
Crew:	1	

Bug

This junior trainer produced by Performance Laser, doubles as a tender. The design has the versatility to take an adult and two children when sailing, and a lot more as a tender. The boat is mass-produced in polyethylene, weighs only 110lb (46kg) and has the option of a standard or racing rig.

Length:	8.5ft	2.6m
Beam:	4.25ft	1.3m
Mainsail:		
Standard	41sq.ft	5.3sq.m
Racing	57sq.ft	5.3sq.m
Mast:		
Standard	12.5ft	3.84m
Racing	15ft	4.47m
Weight:	110lb	46kg
Crew:	1 adult + 2 children	

Pico

This entry-level beach dinghy can be sailed singlehanded or two-up, and is available with a standard or racing rig. Mass-produced by Performance Laser in polyethylene, the boat has a self-draining cockpit and weighs 198lb (90kg).

Length:	11.5ft	3.5m
Beam:	4.75ft	1.43m
Mainsail:		
Standard	55sq.ft	5.14sq.m
Racing	68sq.ft	6.33sq.m
Mast:	18ft	5.54m
Weight:	198lb	90kg
Crew:	1–2	

● SINGLEHANDERS

Topper

The Topper was the first mass-production dinghy utilising an automated injection moulding system. Since its introduction in 1977, more than 50,000 have been produced. They are popular for both sail training and racing and were designed to be carried on the top of a car. The boat has two sizes of mainsail, the smaller is used for sail training and racing in strong winds.

Length:	11.1ft	3.38m
Beam:	3.75ft	1.12m
Mainsail:		
Small	45.2sq.ft	4.2sq.m
Standard	57sq.ft	5.3sq.m
Mast:	11ft	3.35m
Weight:	94lb	43kg
Crew:	1–2	

Topper Topaz Uno Plus

Another popular beach boat which is available injection moulded in polypropylene or moulded in glass-reinforced plastic. It is an ideal training boat that can be sailed by every member of the family, either two-up or singlehanded and has the option of a jib and asymmetric spinnaker.

Length:		12.6ft	3.86m
Beam:		4.75ft	1.45m
Mainsail:			
	Standard	60.7sq.ft	5.64sq.m
	Racing	74.6sq.ft	6.93sq.m
Jib:		18.8sq.ft	1.75sq.m
Asymmetric spinnaker:		86.1sq.m	8sq.m
Mast:		18.37ft	5.60m
Weight:		132lb	60kg
Crew:		1–2	

Rs Tera

Another popular injection moulded polypropylene beach dinghy, designed for entry-level sailing. The boat is raced singlehanded, but quite capable of carrying two people when used for training and tuition. It also doubles as a rowing tender.

Length:	9.5ft	2.87m
Beam:	4ft	1.23m
Mainsail:		
Small	38.2sq.ft	3.7sq.m
Racing	50sq.ft	4.8sq.m
Mast:	13.7ft	4.18m
Weight:	86lb	39kg
Crew:	1–2	

Laser

The laser is a one-design singlehander with three sizes of rig allowing youngsters to progress their levels of competence and competition right up to Olympic level without changing boat. With 200,000 sailing worldwide, the car-toppable Laser is one of the most popular classes.

Length:	13.78ft	4.2m
Beam:	4.56ft	1.39m
Mainsail:		
4.7	50.6sq.ft	4.7sq.m
Radial	62sq.ft	5.76sq.m
Olympic	76sq.ft	7.06sq.m
Mast:	19.35ft	5.9m
Weight:	130lb	59kg
Crew:	1	

⬤ GENERAL-PURPOSE DINGHIES

Laser Bahia

This general-purpose family polyethylene dinghy can be sailed, motored or rowed, and makes an ideal first family dinghy to learn to sail in, with room enough for 2–3 crew and an instructor. It even has a removable cool box that can be carried in the stern for picnics on the beach. At a later stage, the boat can be upgraded to include a spinnaker and trapeze for racing.

Length:	15ft	4.6m
Beam:	6ft	1.8m
Mainsail:	113sq.ft	10.5sq.m
Jib:	40sq.ft	3.75sq.m
Asymmetric spinnaker:	150sq.ft	14sq.m
Mast:	20.5ft	6.29m
Weight:	386lb	175kg
Crew:	2–5	

Rs Vision

Another good family orientated general-purpose polyethylene dinghy with plenty of stowage space that can be sailed motored or rowed. This design is the same overall length as the Bahia, but with a narrower beam and smaller rig, she is significantly lighter to manhandle. The boat has the option of an asymmetric spinnaker.

Length:	15ft	4.6m
Beam:	5.7ft	1.75m
Mainsail:	95sq.ft	9.2sq.m
Jib:	33sq.ft	3.2sq.m
Asymmetric spinnaker:	130sq.ft	12sq.m
Mast:	21.65ft	6.6m
Weight:	275lb	125kg
Crew:	2–4	

● CATAMARANS

Topper Topaz 12

The Topaz 12 is a polyethylene-produced beach catamaran designed specifically to introduce youngsters to catamaran sailing at as early an age as possible. It is the smallest in the Topper range that also includes 14ft (4.26m) and 16ft (4.87m) versions. The Topaz 12 can be upgraded to include a spinnaker and trapeze as experience increases.

Length:	11.9ft	3.63m
Beam:	5.9ft	1.8m
Mainsail:	77.5sq.ft	7.2sq.m
Jib:	19.37sq.ft	1.8sq.m
Asymmetric spinnaker:	175.35sq.ft	7sq.m
Mast:	18.7ft	5.7m
Weight:	187.4lb	85kg
Crew:	1–3	

Dart 16

The Dart 16 is another fun performance catamaran that can be upgraded with a spinnaker and twin trapezes when the time comes to start racing. Like the Topaz, the polyethylene hulls have a skeg at their stern, which negates the need for daggerboards and allows the boat to be sailed straight up the beach.

Length:	15ft	4.64m
Beam:	7.5ft	2.3m
Mainsail:	112sq.ft	10.4sq.m
Jib:	29sq.ft	2.7sq.m
Asymmetric spinnaker:	124sq.ft	11.63sq.m
Mast:	24.5ft	7.5m
Weight:	313lb	142kg
Crew:	1–5	

KEELBOATS

Laser Stratos Keel

The Stratos Keel is an ideal family trailer boat where stability is a key requirement. The design's integral swing keel, weighing 100kg, allows the boat to be launched and retrieved easily from a road trailer, and with the foil raised, she floats in just 6in (15cm) of water. The boat can be motored, rowed and sailed, has a self-draining cockpit and can be left on a mooring.

Length:	16.2ft	4.94m
Beam:	6.56ft	2m
Mainsail:	119.6sq.ft	11.11sq.m
Jib:	36.8sq.ft	3.42sq.m
Asymmetric spinnaker:	135sq.ft	12.54sq.m
Mast:	23.3ft	7.1m
Weight:	419lb	190kg
Keel:	220lb	100kg
Crew:	1–6	

4. LEARNING TO SAIL

PARTS OF THE BOAT

There is no need to get too bogged down with nautical terms at this stage, but it helps to know the various parts of a dinghy and what they do.

Mainsail
Sail attached to mast and boom.

Boom vang (gnav)
Multi-purchase system controlling downward tension on the boom.

Jib fairlead
Adjustable lead for rope that controls the jib or headsail.

Tiller extension
Attached to the tiller by a universal joint, this extends the reach of the tiller to allow the helmsman to sit out and control the rudder from the side deck.

Side deck/buoyancy tank
Seats that double as side buoyancy.

Port side
Left-hand side of the boat.

Gunwale
*(pronounced 'gunel')
Top edge of the boat.*

Cockpit
Crew area within the boat.

Toe straps
To hook your feet under when sitting on the side deck.

Stern/transom
Back end of the dinghy.

Tiller
Used to steer the boat.

Transom drains
Holes in transom to allow water to escape the cockpit after a capsize or flooding.

Removable rudder
Foil to steer the dinghy, which pivots up when boat is being launched or beached.

Hull
Outer shell of the boat.

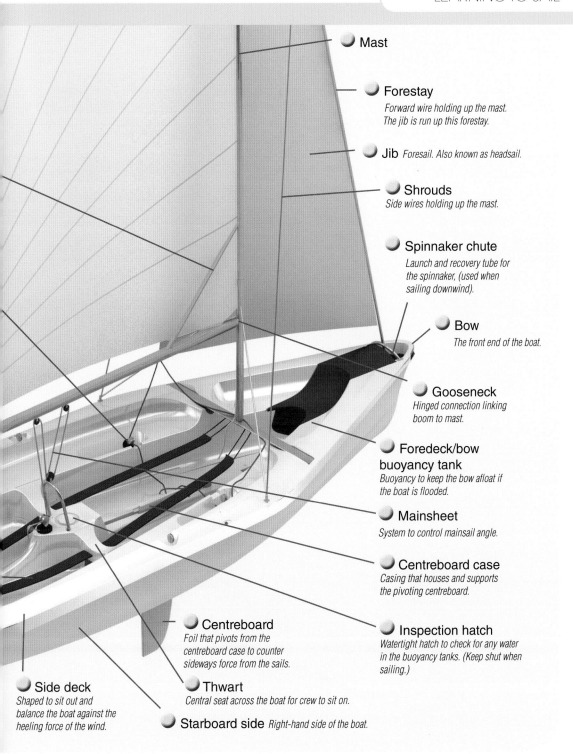

Mast

Forestay
Forward wire holding up the mast. The jib is run up this forestay.

Jib Foresail. Also known as headsail.

Shrouds
Side wires holding up the mast.

Spinnaker chute
Launch and recovery tube for the spinnaker, (used when sailing downwind).

Bow
The front end of the boat.

Gooseneck
Hinged connection linking boom to mast.

Foredeck/bow buoyancy tank
Buoyancy to keep the bow afloat if the boat is flooded.

Mainsheet
System to control mainsail angle.

Centreboard case
Casing that houses and supports the pivoting centreboard.

Centreboard
Foil that pivots from the centreboard case to counter sideways force from the sails.

Inspection hatch
Watertight hatch to check for any water in the buoyancy tanks. (Keep shut when sailing.)

Side deck
Shaped to sit out and balance the boat against the heeling force of the wind.

Thwart
Central seat across the boat for crew to sit on.

Starboard side Right-hand side of the boat.

SINGLEHANDERS

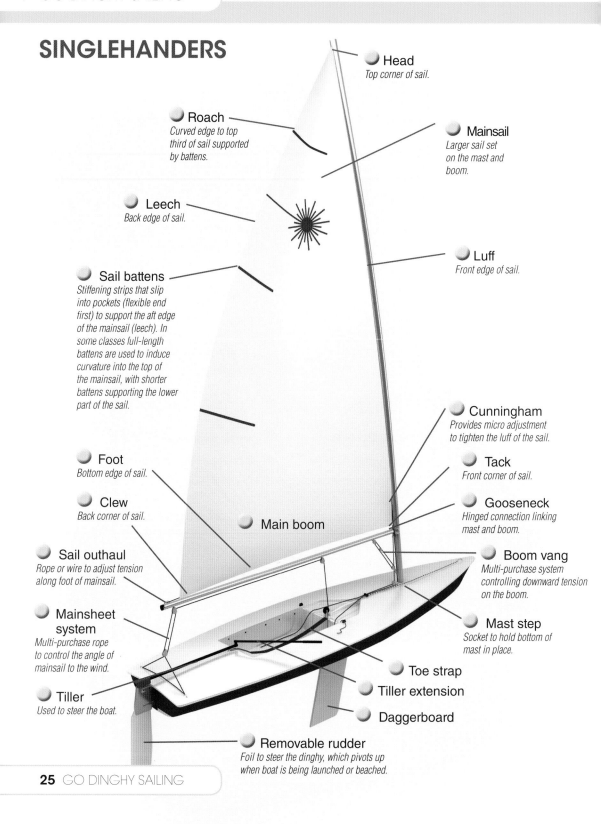

Head
Top corner of sail.

Roach
Curved edge to top third of sail supported by battens.

Mainsail
Larger sail set on the mast and boom.

Leech
Back edge of sail.

Luff
Front edge of sail.

Sail battens
Stiffening strips that slip into pockets (flexible end first) to support the aft edge of the mainsail (leech). In some classes full-length battens are used to induce curvature into the top of the mainsail, with shorter battens supporting the lower part of the sail.

Cunningham
Provides micro adjustment to tighten the luff of the sail.

Foot
Bottom edge of sail.

Tack
Front corner of sail.

Clew
Back corner of sail.

Gooseneck
Hinged connection linking mast and boom.

Main boom

Sail outhaul
Rope or wire to adjust tension along foot of mainsail.

Boom vang
Multi-purchase system controlling downward tension on the boom.

Mainsheet system
Multi-purchase rope to control the angle of mainsail to the wind.

Mast step
Socket to hold bottom of mast in place.

Toe strap

Tiller
Used to steer the boat.

Tiller extension

Daggerboard

Removable rudder
Foil to steer the dinghy, which pivots up when boat is being launched or beached.

CATAMARANS

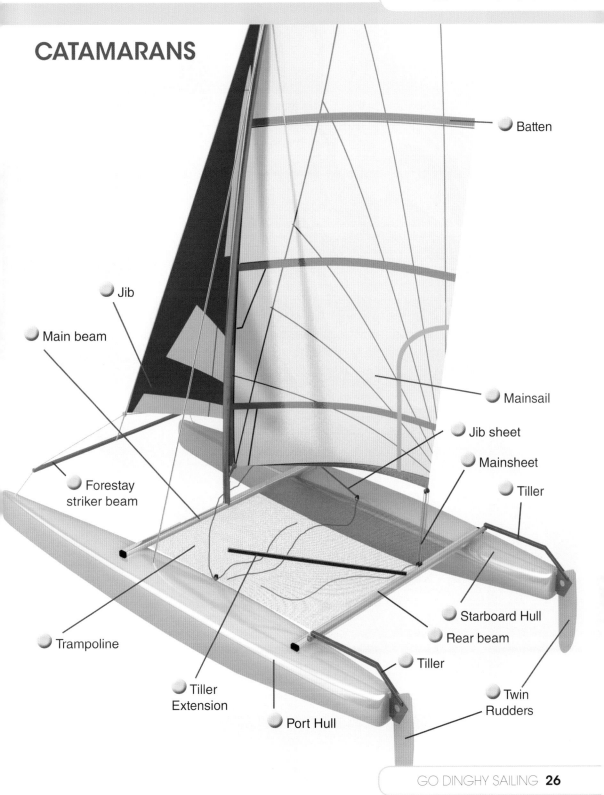

Batten

Jib

Main beam

Mainsail

Jib sheet

Mainsheet

Forestay
striker beam

Tiller

Trampoline

Starboard Hull

Rear beam

Tiller

Tiller
Extension

Twin
Rudders

Port Hull

BASICS OF SAILING

Ever wondered how a heavy jumbo jet stays up in the air? Well it is exactly the same science that gives a sailboat its forward power. This simple experiment best explains the theory.

Hold a spoon lightly under a running tap. You might expect the flow to push the spoon away, but in fact, the bowl is sucked into the flow of water. It is the same with air flowing round the wing of a plane and the sail of a boat. Air flowing around the outer curved surface (leeward side) travels faster than round than on the inner (windward) side. This causes a pressure differential on the two sides of the foil with higher pressure on the windward side than the leeward one. The force created by this pressure differential pulls the sail to leeward just like the spoon is sucked into the flow of water. It acts almost at right angles to the sail, with part of it driving the boat forwards, the rest pushing it sideways.

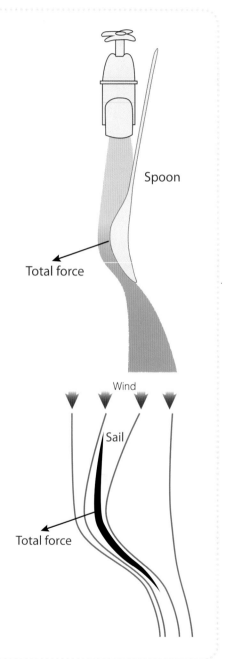

Spoon

Total force

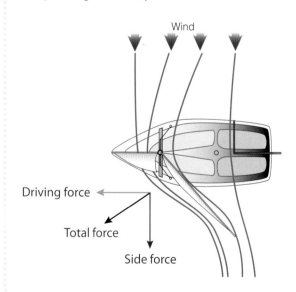

Wind

Driving force

Total force

Side force

Wind

Sail

Total force

SAIL TRIM

A sail works at its optimum when the leading edge (luff) is set at a particular angle to the wind. Not pulled in (sheeted in) enough, and the sail will flap; sheeted in too hard and it will produce more side force than forward power. The angle is critical, but there is a simple way to find it. Simply pull the sheet (rope) in until the luff stops fluttering, then continue to play the sheet, pulling it in and out slowly to keep the luff on the point of flutter. You will need to adjust the sheet to match the angle of wind with each change of course, progressively letting the sail out, the further you bear away from the eye of the wind (see points of sail page 36).

Most multi-crewed dinghies have two sails; a forward sail called a jib, and the mainsail. The jib induces a 'slot effect' rather like the 'flaps' on the trailing edge of a plane wing when they are extended out to increase 'lift for take off and landing' at slower air speeds. The airflow narrows and accelerates through the 'slot' between the jib and mainsail, and enhances the pressure differential between the windward and leeward sides of the mainsail.

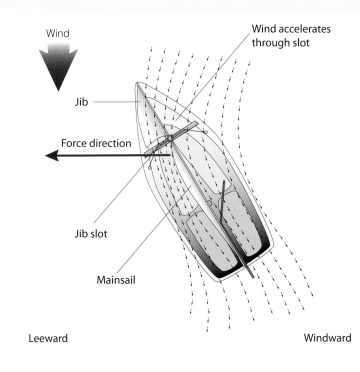

Wind

Wind accelerates through slot

Jib

Force direction

Jib slot

Mainsail

Leeward

Windward

TRIMMING SAILS

Modern sails have telltales – thin strips of nylon cloth or wool attached on each side of the sail to indicate the pressure differential. The sail is in trim when the two telltales are streaming back close together. If the telltale on the leeward side (back side of the sail) rises upwards, ❶ this is a sign to let the sail out a little. If the windward (front side of the sail) telltale rises upwards, ❸ then the sail needs to be pulled in.

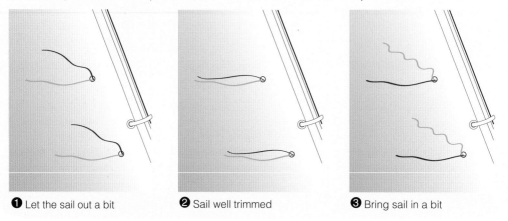

❶ Let the sail out a bit   ❷ Sail well trimmed   ❸ Bring sail in a bit

WHAT PART DOES THE KEEL PLAY?

Without a keel (or in the case of a dinghy, its centreboard or daggerboard pushed down under the boat) the force of the wind would simply push the boat sideways and it would crab across the water. The keel, and to a lesser extent the rudder, produces an opposite force to that on the sail and by cancelling this side force, the forward force produced by the sails is enhanced which drives the boat forward.

The closer a boat sails towards the wind, the greater the side force produced by the sails, and thus the greater need for keel area to resist this. However, the further away a boat sails from the eye of the wind, the less the side force, which allows for the keel to be raised inside the boat to lessen wetted area and friction. Most dinghies and catamarans are fitted with lifting centreboards or daggerboards so that the keel area can be adjusted to suit the point of sail.

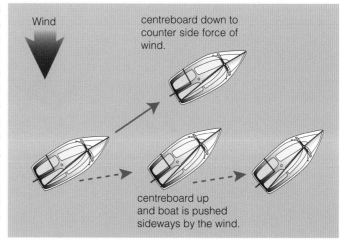

Wind

centreboard down to counter side force of wind.

centreboard up and boat is pushed sideways by the wind.

CREW WEIGHT

Crew weight is needed to balance out the heeling force of the wind against the resisting force of the keel. In a dinghy, the position of the crew sitting on the windward side (opposite side to the sails) stops the boat from capsizing. Keelboats, on the other hand, rely on the heavy weight of the keel to balance out this heeling effect, though crew positioning to balance the boat is just as important for efficient forward movement.

DRIVING FORCE OF THE WIND

Sailing to windward close-hauled

The lateral force of the wind on the sails is countered by the sideways resistance generated by the keel and crew weight to balance out the heeling force. This leads to a forward force that will drive the boat to within 40° of the eye of the wind. Sails are pulled in taught.

Sailing across the wind

This is the most efficient angle of sail and is termed 'reaching'. The lateral force of the wind is reduced and the forward, driving force of the wind is increased. Sails are let out approximately half way.

Running downwind

This is sailing away from the wind. All the wind force goes into pushing the boat forward. Sails are let right out.

CLOSE-HAULED: SAILING BETWEEN 40°–45° FROM THE WIND
This is beating to windward. The centreboard needs to be fully down, sails sheeted in hard and crew weight positioned on the windward side to balance the boat.

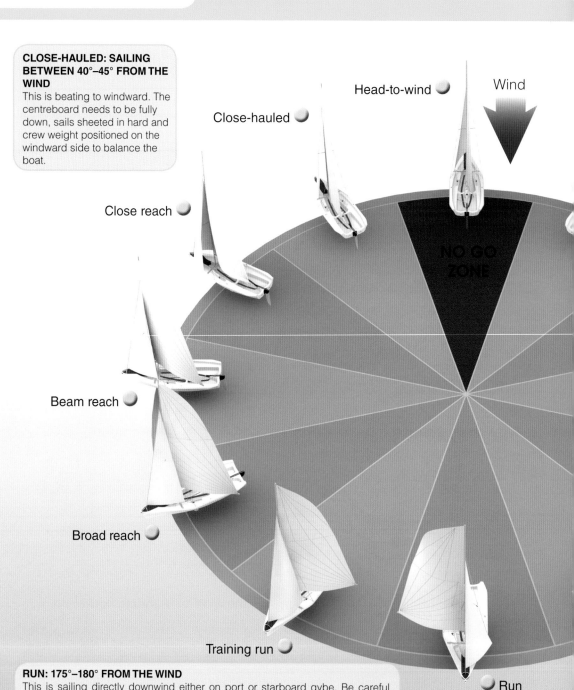

Head-to-wind

Wind

Close-hauled

NO GO ZONE

Close reach

Beam reach

Broad reach

Training run

Run

RUN: 175°–180° FROM THE WIND
This is sailing directly downwind either on port or starboard gybe. Be careful not to pass the stern of the boat through the eye of the wind as the mainsail will slam across in what is termed an involuntary gybe. Let the sails right out. The jib can be set on opposite side to the mainsail to present the greatest sail area to the wind. Centreboard is fully raised and crew weight is spread across the boat.

HEAD TO WIND
This is when you are facing the eye of the wind. This no-go zone extends to 45° either side. Turn too high into wind and the sails will flap, the boat will stall and the wind will push you backwards. It is not possible to sail directly into the wind. The only way to make progress is to sail a zigzag course 45° either side of the wind with sails pulled in hard. Each change from one side of the wind to the other is called a tack. The zigzag course is termed beating to windward.

Close-hauled

Close reach

CLOSE REACH: 50°–80° FROM THE WIND
Ease sails out a quarter of the way, raise the centreboard a quarter, and continue to balance the boat with your weight.

BEAM REACH: 90° FROM THE WIND
Ease sails out half way, raise the centreboard half way, and continue to balance the boat with your weight.

Beam reach

BROAD REACH: 120°–160° FROM THE WIND
This is the fastest point of sail. Ease sails out three-quarters of the way, raise the centreboard three-quarters up, move crew weight further aft and continue to balance the boat.

Broad reach

POINTS OF SAIL

Keep a close eye on where the wind is coming from. Look around to see which way flags are flying and get used to sensing the wind direction on your face. Whenever you change course in relation to the wind, you must change the set of the sails, height of centreboard and crews positions to match the dinghy's balance and heading to the wind.

Training run

TRAINING RUN: 170° FROM THE WIND
This is the safest angle for beginners to sail downwind. Any further away from the wind and you run the risk of an involuntary gybe. Let the sails right out, fully raise the centreboard and spread crew weight across the boat.

FIVE ESSENTIALS TO SAILING

There are five key essentials to remember when sailing a boat. They are all inter-related, so when one factor changes, check that the other four are right.

1. Sail trim

Keep a constant eye on sail trim, the optimum angle sails need to be set to the wind, to maximise their performance. Watch the telltales, or gradually ease and tighten the sheets to keep the luff of the sails on the point of beginning to flutter. This will give you maximum efficiency. The wind is constantly changing, even when you maintain a straight course, so the sails need to be adjusted all the time to suit.

Wind

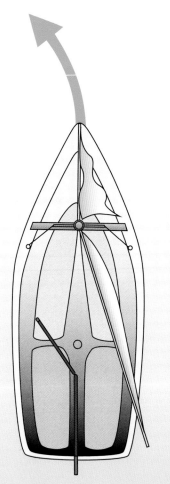
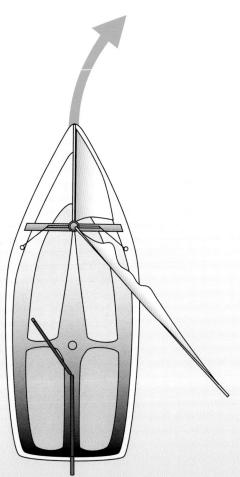

2. Centreboard

This needs to be adjusted to suit the changing side force exerted by the wind on the sails. Sailing upwind, this needs to be fully down, then eased up by an increasing amount the more you bear away from the eye of the wind. This reduces water resistance on the boat and helps to increase speed. The board should be half up on a broad reach across the wind, and fully up when running before the wind.

On keelboats, the keel is fixed and cannot be adjusted unless the boat is fitted with a swing keel.

TIP

The difference between tacking and gybing

Tacking is when you change course while sailing upwind, and turn the bows through the eye of the wind.

Gybing is when you change course while sailing downwind, and turn the stern through the eye of the wind.

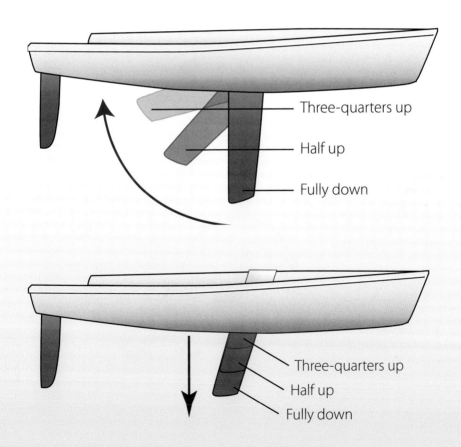

Three-quarters up

Half up

Fully down

Three-quarters up

Half up

Fully down

3. Balance

Boats sail fastest when kept upright, so crew weight is the most important factor when balancing the boat. When sailing upwind, the crew need to sit out on the windward side to counter the heeling force of the wind. The heeling force reduces the further you sail away from the wind to the point when sailing directly downwind, the crew sits on the opposite side to the helmsman to counter each other's weight.

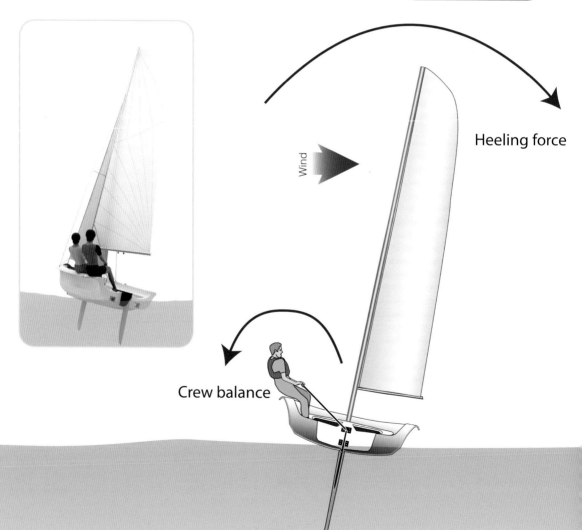

Heeling force

Wind

Crew balance

4. Trim

The boat should be sailed level in a fore-and-aft plane. The helm and crew should sit close to each other to minimise pitching and keep from depressing either the bows or stern in the water. Only when the boat is fast planing on top of the water when broad reaching across the wind should the crew move their weight aft in order to keep the bows from burying into an oncoming wave.

5. Course made good

Keep a constant check on your course, compass and where possible your destination point. If this is directly to windward, you will have to zigzag upwind, tacking through the eye of the wind.

BASIC KNOTS

These are the basic sailing knots. You need to be able to do these with your eyes shut, so carry a piece of cord in your pocket and practice them during quiet moments until they become instinctive.

Bight and loop
The first terms to learn

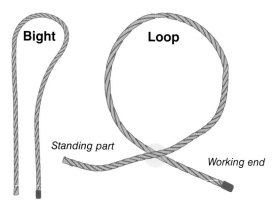

Bight   Loop

Standing part

Working end

Bowline
Use: to form a secure loop in the end of a mooring line to lasso a bollard, or attach a sheet to the clew of a sail.
Remember the rule: The rabbit comes up through the hole, runs round the tree, then goes back down the hole again.

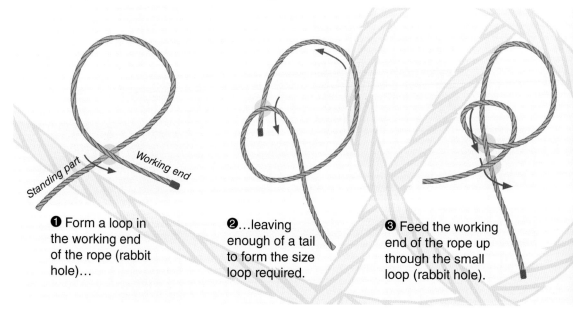

Standing part   Working end

❶ Form a loop in the working end of the rope (rabbit hole)…

❷…leaving enough of a tail to form the size loop required.

❸ Feed the working end of the rope up through the small loop (rabbit hole).

◡ Figure-of-eight knot

Use: stopper knot tied into the end of sail control lines (sheets) to stop them running out through a block or fairlead.

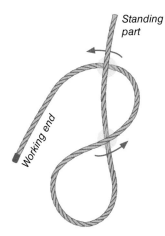

❶ Form a loop.

❷ Pass the working end (tail) round the back of the standing part

❸ Return the standing part through the loop

❹ Pull tight.

❹ Pass it round the back of the standing part (tree)…

❺…and then down through the small loop (rabbit hole).

❻ Pull tight on both working and standing parts of the rope to complete.

Clove hitch

Use: a temporary quick release knot to tie fenders or ropes to a rail or ring.

❶ Pass the working end around the object.

❷ Then back across itself.

❸ Form a second half hitch.

❹ Tuck the working end under itself.

❺ Pull tight.

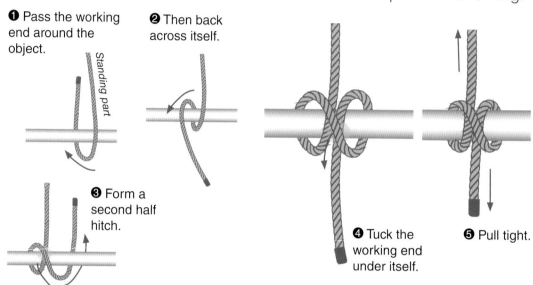

Reef knot

Use: tying two ropes together

Remember this simple rule: Left over right, right over left

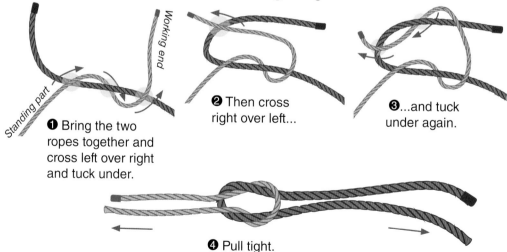

❶ Bring the two ropes together and cross left over right and tuck under.

❷ Then cross right over left...

❸ ...and tuck under again.

❹ Pull tight.

Sheet bend

Use: to join together two ropes of unequal thickness.

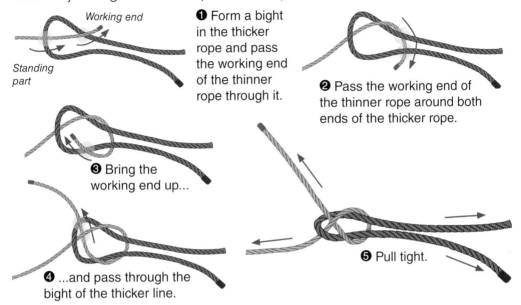

Working end

Standing part

❶ Form a bight in the thicker rope and pass the working end of the thinner rope through it.

❷ Pass the working end of the thinner rope around both ends of the thicker rope.

❸ Bring the working end up...

❹ ...and pass through the bight of the thicker line.

❺ Pull tight.

Cleating a rope

Use: tying off a mooring line or sail halyard on a horn cleat.

Working end

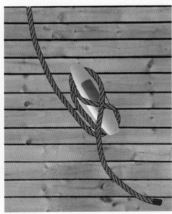

❶ Take a turn round the cleat...

❷... then cross over the working end in a figure-of-eight.

❸ Finish with a further turn around the cleat to allow for a quick release.

�𝅘 Coiling rope

Use: to tidy loose ends of rope ready to shake out at a moment's notice.

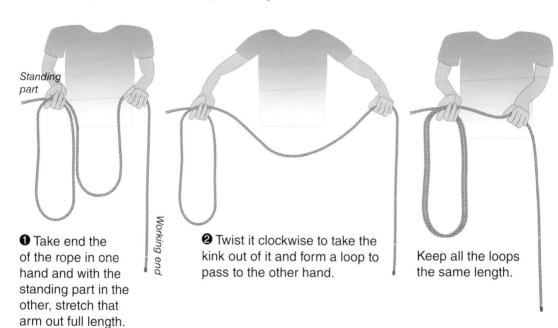

Standing part

Working end

❶ Take end the of the rope in one hand and with the standing part in the other, stretch that arm out full length.

❷ Twist it clockwise to take the kink out of it and form a loop to pass to the other hand.

Keep all the loops the same length.

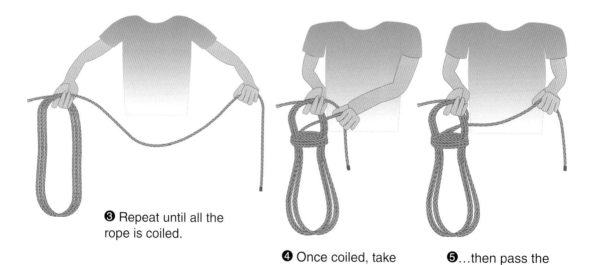

❸ Repeat until all the rope is coiled.

❹ Once coiled, take the working end and loop around the coils a couple of times…

❺…then pass the end through the top end of the coil and pull tight.

◔ Round turn and two half hitches

Use: A secure knot used to tie a mooring line to a post or ring.

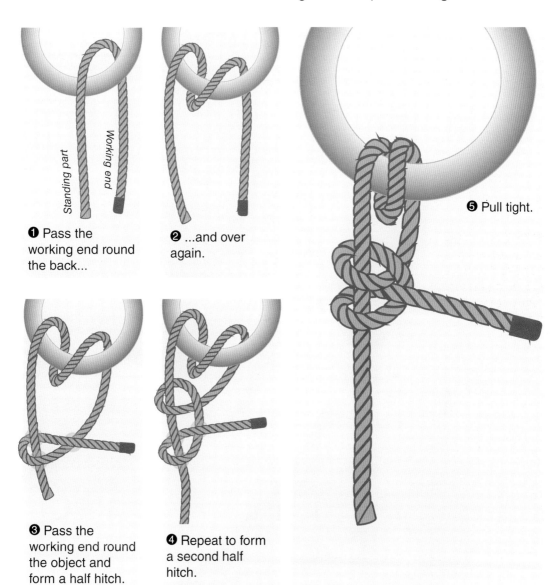

Standing part

Working end

❶ Pass the working end round the back...

❷ ...and over again.

❺ Pull tight.

❸ Pass the working end round the object and form a half hitch.

❹ Repeat to form a second half hitch.

5. GETTING AFLOAT

CLOTHING AND SAFETY EQUIPMENT

Stay warm, stay dry, stay comfortable

Sailing is fun, so don't allow the conditions to dampen the experience. Modern sailing clothing is designed to keep you warm and dry, and give you the freedom of movement to move quickly around the boat.

If you are sailing in a hot climate, then the waters will invariably be warm too so you may not require anything more than a bathing costume and buoyancy aid, but take a waterproof top with you – just in case.

In non-tropical waters, it is often colder afloat than on land and you need to dress accordingly. Once you get cold in a dinghy it is difficult to get warm again. Plan on wearing a set of waterproofs over thermal or fleece undergarments. Alternatively, if you know you are going to get wet, then consider wearing a wetsuit with a waterproof top to guard against wind chill.

If you are taking first lessons at a sailing school, then you will invariably be provided with the clothing and safety equipment you need. If not, waterproof jacket and trousers, non-slip sports shoes and a buoyancy aid should suffice for your introductory sail. As you advance to faster boats when spray and the possibilities of a capsize become more of an issue, consider wearing a 'breathable' dry suit which has rubber ankle, neck and wrist seals to keep the water out.

Non-slip boots, fingerless gloves to stop the ropes cutting into your hands, and a hat may also prove to be essential. A hat is certainly so in cold weather because 30% of body heat is lost through the head.

● Safety equipment

A buoyancy aid or personal flotation device (PFD) is a must, and is as important as 'belting up' in a car. As their name implies, these are aids, not life savers, but popular with dinghy sailors because they are far less restrictive than a full-blown lifejacket. These vests are designed simply to keep you afloat in the event of a capsize, so non-swimmers should always wear a lifejacket which is designed to turn the wearer onto their back and keep their head above water.

RIGGING THE BOAT

The methods for connecting and attaching the sails varies from one boat to another, though the principles remain the same. If your first sailing experience is with a school, the instructor will show you how.

● Parts of a mainsail ● Parts of a jib

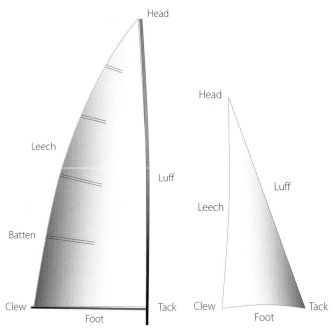

● Connecting the sails

Make sure you always turn the dinghy head to wind before hoisting the sails.

In some classes, the mast and boom have black bands at their extremities to mark the extremities that the mainsail can be stretched to. Extending the sails beyond these marks breaches the measurement rules, so keep the sail within these bands.

CONNECTING THE JIB

❶ Attach the jib tack to the bow.

CONNECTING THE MAINSAIL

❶ Insert the battens (thin end first) into their respective pockets.

❹ Connect the tack to the inner end of the boo

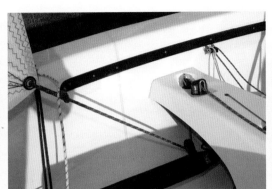

❷ Attach the sheets to the clew.

❸ Lead the sheets through fairleads on each side.

❹ Attach the jib halyard to the head.

❷ Attach the clew to the boom outhaul, sliding the bolt rope into the boom track if sail is not loose footed.

❸ Tension the clew outhaul. This controls the shape of the sail. Do not stretch beyond black band limits.

❺ Attach the main halyard to the head of the mainsail.

❻ Slide the head and bolt rope into the slot in the back of the mast ready to hoist.

HOISTING THE SAILS

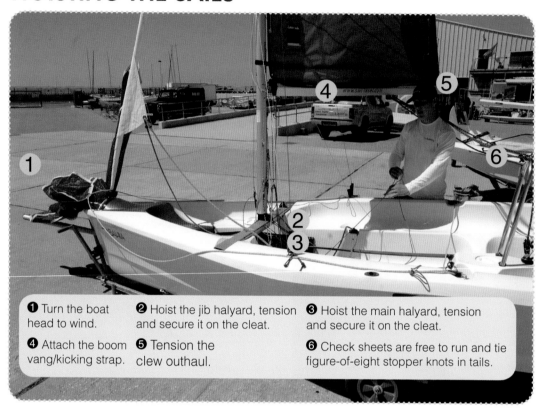

❶ Turn the boat head to wind.

❷ Hoist the jib halyard, tension and secure it on the cleat.

❸ Hoist the main halyard, tension and secure it on the cleat.

❹ Attach the boom vang/kicking strap.

❺ Tension the clew outhaul.

❻ Check sheets are free to run and tie figure-of-eight stopper knots in tails.

RIGGING A SINGLEHANDER

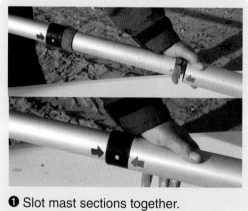

❶ Slot mast sections together.

❷ Slide the sleeved luff down the mast.

❸ Attach the boom to the mast gooseneck and attach the clew outhaul.

❹ Tension the clew outhaul and tie it off.

❺ Insert the battens thin end first into their respective pockets.

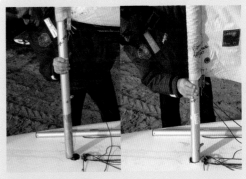

❻ Insert the mast foot in its hole on the foredeck.

❼ Connect the vang to the boom.

❽ Connect the mainsheet, tie a figure-of-eight stopper knot in the tail, then attach the rudder and daggerboard.

REEFING

If the winds are strong, it may be prudent to reduce sail area. Most singlehanders are reefed by rolling the sail around the mast.

With two-person boats, it is often possible to roll the foot of the mainsail around the boom, or in the event of having a centre mainsheet, rolling the sail up, tying it along the boom, and connecting the boom to a second tack and clew higher up the sail (as in this picture).

Una-rigged mainsail reefed by rolling it around the mast.

RIGGING – CATAMARAN

❶ Get the sails out of their bag.

❷ Feed the mainsail luff into the slot in the mast.

❸ Tension, then tie off the halyards and roller furl the jib.

❹ Place the launching cradle underneath the boat...

❺ ...then lift the boat and push the cradle under until the boat is balanced.

❻ Fit the rudders, attach the sheets...and you are ready to go sailing!

LAUNCHING

1 Tie the bow to the trolley so that it won't sail away.

2 Keeping the boat head to wind, push or pull the boat to the water's edge.

3 Fit the rudder.

CHECK:

4 That the bungs are in and the transom flaps are shut.

5 That sails are hoisted correctly, sheets are free to run and vang is tensioned.

6 That you have a paddle to hand.

7 That your buoyancy aid is worn correctly.

THEN:

8 Wheel the boat into the water still facing into wind.

9 Once afloat, untie the bow line.

10 One crew holds the bow head to wind…

11 …while the other pulls the trolley clear and park it out of the way.

YOU ARE READY TO PUSH OFF.

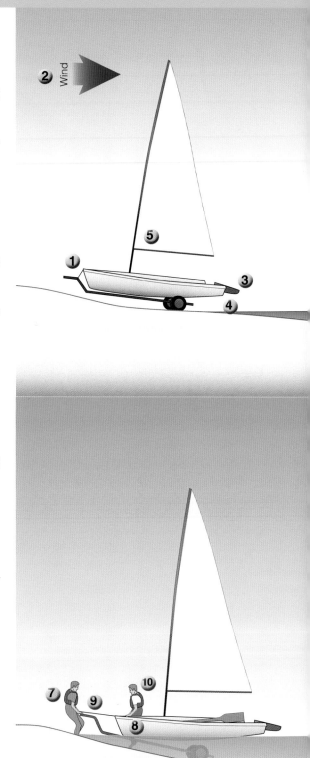

6. FIRST STEPS

STARTING AND STOPPING

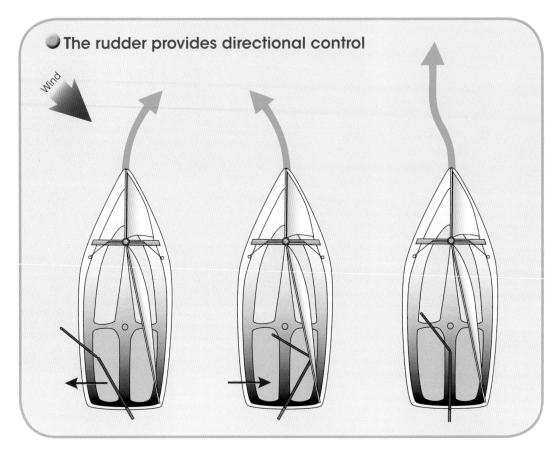

● **The rudder provides directional control**

Wind

1.
Pull the tiller towards you and the boat will point away from the wind and speed will increase. This is called bearing away.

2.
Push the tiller away and the boat will turn up into wind and stop. This is termed luffing up into wind.

3.
Steer towards a distant point and practice steering a gentle 'S' course. You will soon find that you start steering instinctively.

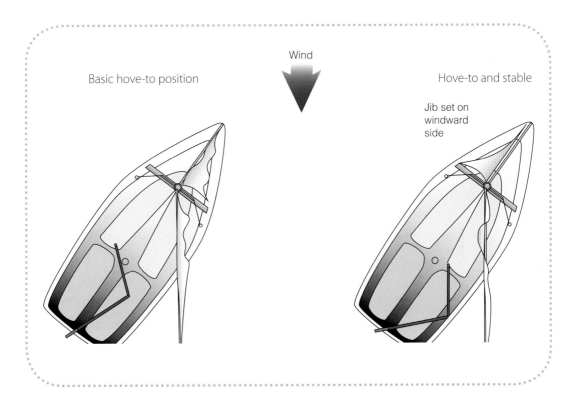

Basic hove-to position

Wind

Hove-to and stable

Jib set on windward side

◖ Stopping

Let the sheets to the jib and mainsail run free so that the sails flap.

As the dinghy slows, helm pushes the tiller away to steer the bows up towards the wind. This is termed the basic hove-to position.

To stop the boat for a longer period, the helm keeps the tiller pushed away and the crew pulls the jib round to the windward side and cleats the sheet hard in.

The rudder now counters the force on the jib and the boat will remain calm and stable, balanced at a close reach angle to the wind.

To resume sailing, the crew have only to release the jib, sheet it in on the opposite side until the sail fills, and the helm bears away and trims the mainsail to suit the new course.

REACHING, RUNNING AND SAILING CLOSE-HAULED

The first move to learn is sailing from a beam reach (at 90° across the wind) to a training run (170° to the wind) and letting the sails out accordingly.

Practice turning from beam reach to broad reach and then to training run, progressively easing the sails so that their telltales remain streaming parallel.

If you have the sea room, push the tiller away from you to point the boat up closer to the wind, and then sheet in the sails to resume a broad reach course. Practice this manoeuvre again until you feel confident.

When you are happy with this or the waters become limited, turn from training run to close-hauled by pushing the tiller away to turn the boat up until the bows are 45° to the wind, sheet the sails in hard and push the centreboard right down. Be ready to sit on the windward side to balance the heeling force of the wind on the sails.

Practice this combined manoeuvre until both helm and crew are entirely happy with the procedures. You now have a handle on the basics of sailing.

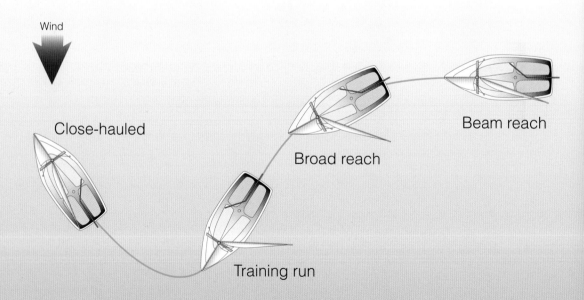

Wind

Close-hauled

Beam reach

Broad reach

Training run

LEARNING TO TACK

Tacking with a centre mainsheet boat

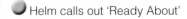 Helm calls out 'Ready About'

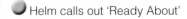 Helm and crew check that sheets are free to run…
…and check that you are clear of other boats around you.

Crew calls 'Ready' and uncleats the jib sheet

Helm then calls 'Lee-ho'…and pushes tiller away without changing hands on tiller

Crew moves inboard and releases the jib sheet as bows turn through the eye of the wind.

Helm and crew move across the boat still facing forward, remembering to duck under the boom.

❶ Helm calls 'Ready about'. Helm and crew check that it is clear to tack. Crew calls 'Ready'.

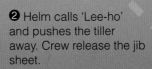

❷ Helm calls 'Lee-ho' and pushes the tiller away. Crew release the jib sheet.

❸ Boat is now head to wind. Helm and crew duck under the boom to opposite side.

⚪ Helm is now steering with his/her tiller hand behind their back and holding the mainsheet in the other hand.

⚪ Helm and crew now move across to balance the boat on the opposite side.

⚪ Crew pulls in the jib sheet

⚪ Helm now straightens the tiller to steer new course and transfers tiller and mainsheet in his hands.

⚪ Helm and crew now adjust the sails to match the course.

Wind

❻ Helm and crew balance the boat and trim the sails to suit new course

❺ Helm swaps tiller and mainsheet in his/her hands and centres the rudder to maintain new course.

❹ Helm is now holding tiller extension in left hand, behind his back, and holding sheet in his right hand. Crew pulls in jib sheet on opposite side.

LEARNING TO TACK
Tacking with an aft mainsheet

⬤ Helm calls out 'Ready About'.

⬤ Helm and crew check that sheets are free to run…
…and that you are clear of other boats around you.

⬤ Crew calls 'Ready' and uncleats the jib sheet.

⬤ Helm then calls 'Lee-ho'…
… pushes tiller away and changes hands on tiller.

⬤ Crew moves inboard and releases the jib sheet as bows turn through the eye of the wind.

❶ Helm calls 'Ready about'. Helm and crew check that it is clear to tack. Crew calls 'Ready'.

❷ Helm calls 'Lee-ho' and pushes the tiller over, changing hands on the tiller as he/she does so. Crew releases the jib sheet.

⬤ Helm and crew move across the boat, crew still facing forward and helm facing aft, remembering to duck under the boom.

⬤ Helm and crew now move across to balance the boat on the opposite side.

⬤ Crew pulls in the jib sheet.

⬤ Helm now straightens the tiller to steer new course. Helm and crew now adjust the sails to match the course.

Wind

❺ Helm centres the rudder to maintain new course. Helm and crew balance the boat and trim the sails to suit new course.

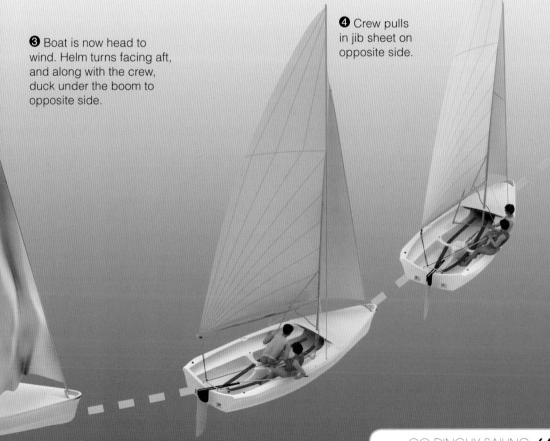

❸ Boat is now head to wind. Helm turns facing aft, and along with the crew, duck under the boom to opposite side.

❹ Crew pulls in jib sheet on opposite side.

GYBING
Gybing a centre mainsheet

Gybing is the equivalent of tacking downwind with the stern instead of the bow passing through the eye of the wind.

1 Starting from a training run, helm calls 'Ready to gybe'.

2 Helm and crew check that it is clear to gybe. Crew checks that centreboard is fully raised, and then calls 'Yes'.

3 Helm calls 'Gybe-ho' and pulls the tiller towards him/her.

4 As boat turns through the eye of the wind, helm and crew remain facing forward. Crew grabs the vang/kicking strap and pulls the boom

5 Helm sets new course and helm and crew adjust sails accordingly.

4 Helm and crew move across to balance the boat on new gybe. Helm swaps tiller hands.

3 As stern passes through the eye of the wind, crew 'assists' the boom across by pulling on the vang/kicking strap. Helm centres the tiller momentarily to take the 'sting' out of the gybe. Helm and crew (both facing forward) duck as the boom swings across.

across. Helm centres the tiller momentarily to take the 'sting' out of the gybe.

5 Helm and crew move across to balance the boat, the helm now steering with hand behind his/her back.

6 Once on the weather side, helm swaps tiller hand. Helm steers new course and crew adjusts the jib to match.

Wind

❶ Helm sheets in mainsail to stop boom from touching shroud and calls 'Ready to gybe'.

❷ Crew checks that centreboard is fully raised, and then calls back 'Yes'.
Helm checks that it is clear to gybe and calls 'Gybe-ho' then pulls tiller towards them to bear way.

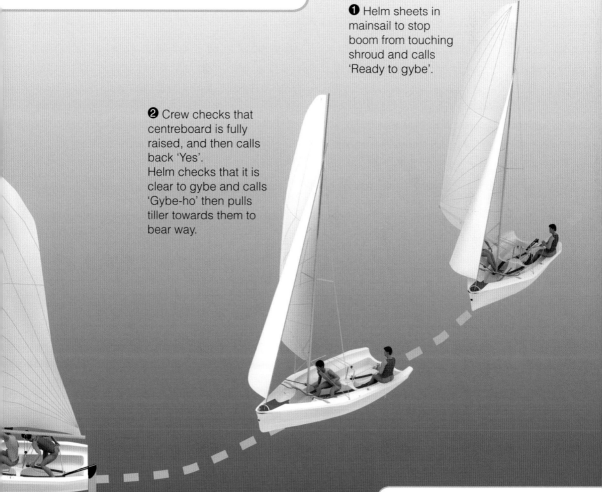

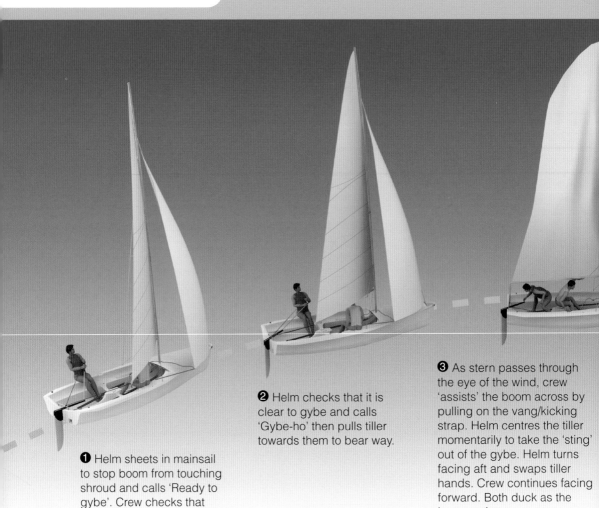

❷ Helm checks that it is clear to gybe and calls 'Gybe-ho' then pulls tiller towards them to bear way.

❸ As stern passes through the eye of the wind, crew 'assists' the boom across by pulling on the vang/kicking strap. Helm centres the tiller momentarily to take the 'sting' out of the gybe. Helm turns facing aft and swaps tiller hands. Crew continues facing forward. Both duck as the boom swings across.

❶ Helm sheets in mainsail to stop boom from touching shroud and calls 'Ready to gybe'. Crew checks that centreboard is fully raised, and then calls back 'Yes'.

Wind

GYBING
Gybing an aft mainsheet

① Starting from a training run, helm calls 'Ready to gybe'.

② Helm and crew check that it is clear to gybe. Crew checks that centreboard is fully raised, and then calls 'Yes'.

③ Helm calls 'Gybe-ho' and pulls the tiller towards him/her.

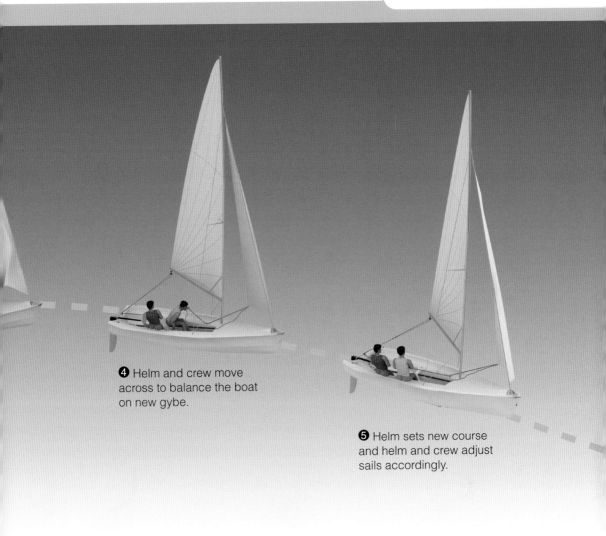

④ Helm and crew move across to balance the boat on new gybe.

⑤ Helm sets new course and helm and crew adjust sails accordingly.

④ As boat turns through the eye of the wind, helm turns facing aft. Crew turns facing forward. Crew grabs the vang/kicking strap and pulls the boom across. Helm centres the tiller momentarily to take the 'sting' out of the gybe and swaps hands on the tiller.

⑤ Helm and crew move across to balance the boat.

⑥ Helm steers new course and crew adjusts the jib to match.

SPINNAKER HANDLING

The time has come to learn how to handle a spinnaker. There are two types of spinnaker; the symmetric reaching/running sail where the luff and leech swap over on port and starboard gybes, and the asymmetric spinnaker (or gennaker as it is sometimes called), which is set from a bowsprit extending out from the bow and is trimmed like a jib.

Symmetric spinnaker

This is set at 90° to the direction of the true wind, the same angle that the spinnaker pole has to be set using the guy and sheet to rotate the sail around the bows of the dinghy.

The two clews are set level to the water in order for the sail to fly to its design shape. This is adjusted by raising or lowering the outer end of the pole which is controlled by adjusting the pole uphaul/downhaul line. If the pole is set too low, then the leading edge of luff of the spinnaker will be too tight. If the pole is set too high, then the luff will be too full and will collapse early.

The only time this rule should be varied is in very light airs when a tight luff will help the spinnaker to set, and in heavy winds when a fuller luff opens the slot between spinnaker and jib or mainsail, and also lessens the heeling force within the sail.

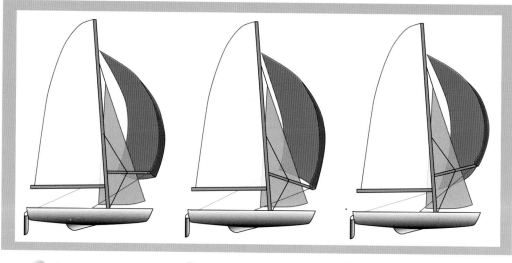

1 Clews set level.   2 Pole set low for light airs.   3 Pole set high for strong winds.

● Dinghy with spinnaker set

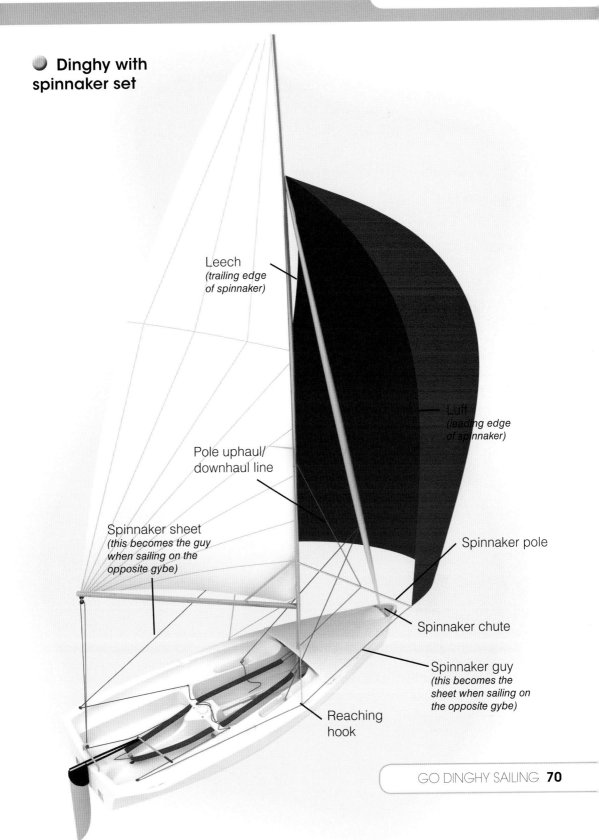

Leech
(trailing edge of spinnaker)

Luff
(leading edge of spinnaker)

Pole uphaul/ downhaul line

Spinnaker sheet
(this becomes the guy when sailing on the opposite gybe)

Spinnaker pole

Spinnaker chute

Spinnaker guy
(this becomes the sheet when sailing on the opposite gybe)

Reaching hook

Setting the spinnaker

Helm turns the boat onto a broad reach or run, straddles the tiller between his/her knees and hoists the spinnaker.

Wind

1 Crew connects outboard end of spinnaker pole to spinnaker sheet, attaches the uphaul/downhaul line, then clips the inboard end of the pole to the mast.

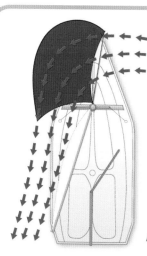

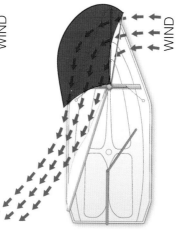

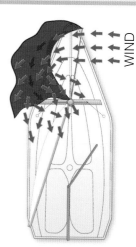

Perfect set: The spinnaker is just curling along the luff and the leech is open enough to maintain laminar flow across the back of the mainsail.

Over-sheeted: Airflow becomes choked at the leach and backwinds the mainsail. This results in greater sideways force at the expense for forward power.

Under-sheeted: The spinnaker collapses and the sail flogs in the wind – no forward power.

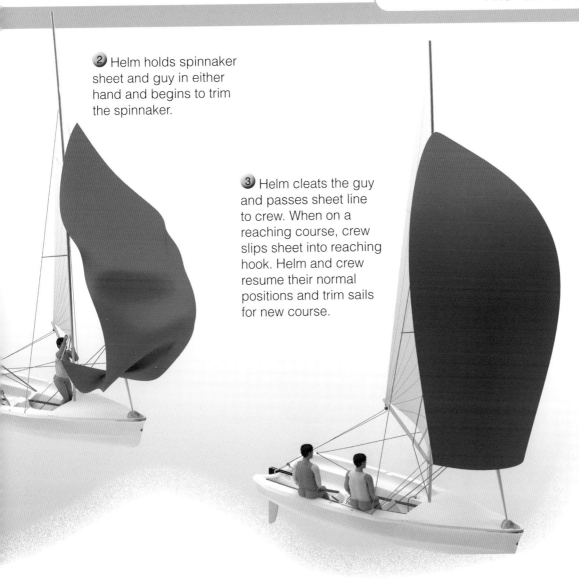

2 Helm holds spinnaker sheet and guy in either hand and begins to trim the spinnaker.

3 Helm cleats the guy and passes sheet line to crew. When on a reaching course, crew slips sheet into reaching hook. Helm and crew resume their normal positions and trim sails for new course.

Spinnaker setting

The spinnaker requires constant adjustment by the crew to keep the luff on the point of curling inwards. Over-sheeted, and the spinnaker will create more side force than forward force. If under-sheeted, the spinnaker will collapse.

Wind

Gybing the spinnaker

1 Helm steers the boat downwind on a training run, straddles the tiller and takes spinnaker sheet and guy in both hands to control spinnaker. Helm calls 'Ready to gybe'. Crew replies 'Yes' and releases the guy from the reaching hook on the windward side.

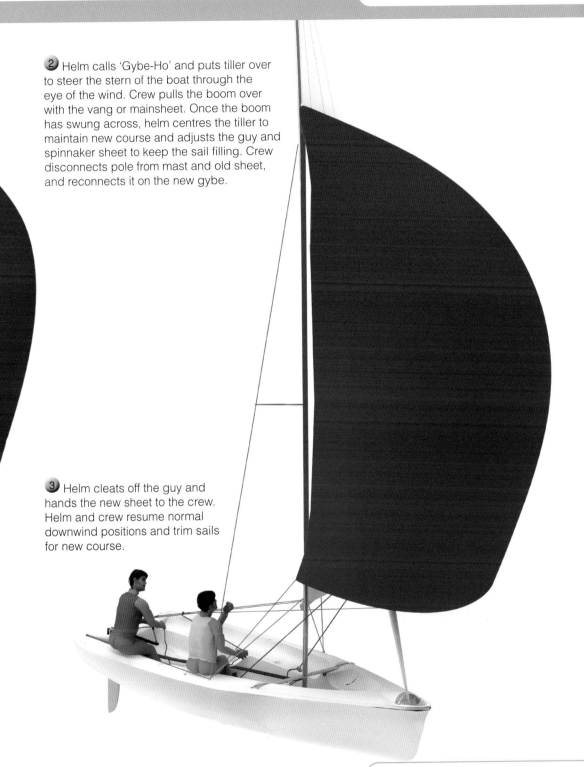

2 Helm calls 'Gybe-Ho' and puts tiller over to steer the stern of the boat through the eye of the wind. Crew pulls the boom over with the vang or mainsheet. Once the boom has swung across, helm centres the tiller to maintain new course and adjusts the guy and spinnaker sheet to keep the sail filling. Crew disconnects pole from mast and old sheet, and reconnects it on the new gybe.

3 Helm cleats off the guy and hands the new sheet to the crew. Helm and crew resume normal downwind positions and trim sails for new course.

Asymmetric spinnakers

Asymmetric spinnakers or gennakers are much simpler to set. They have a single luff, there is no pole or reaching hooks to contend with, and no concerns about keeping the clews level. The sail is controlled just as if it were a jib with double sheets led to either side of the boat. Halyard and downhaul are interconnected so that the bowsprit extends and retracts automatically when the sail is raised or lowered.

GYBING

① Helm calls 'Stand by to gybe'.
Crew replies 'Yes'.

② Helm calls 'Gybe-Ho' and bears off down wind. Crew moves inboard.

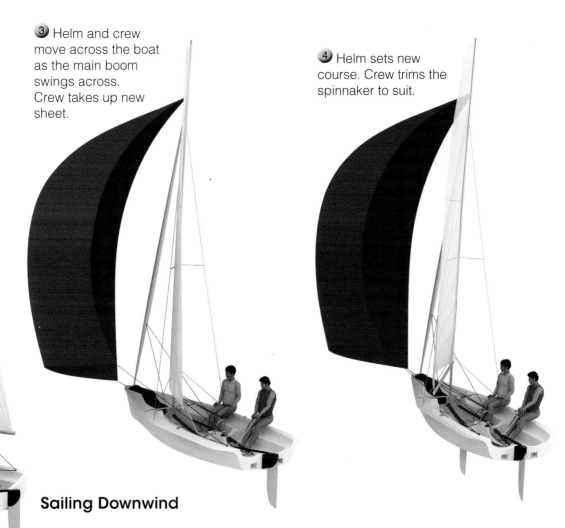

3 Helm and crew move across the boat as the main boom swings across. Crew takes up new sheet.

4 Helm sets new course. Crew trims the spinnaker to suit.

Sailing Downwind

Asymmetric spinnakers are most efficient when reaching, not running downwind, so the fastest course is a zigzag of gybes. These sails generate far more side force than a spinnaker, so dinghies need the centreboard to be fully down.

AVOIDING OTHER BOATS

Just like driving on the road, there are universal right-of-way rules governing boats from the smallest dinghy to the largest ship. These are called the International Regulations for Preventing Collisions at Sea (IRPCS) and they take precedence over any local or racing rules, including those set by the International Sailing Federation (ISAF).

The first rule is to avoid a collision, even if you are right-of-way boat. If you are unsure, then slow or stop the boat by releasing the sheets and turning into wind. Turning away from the wind will only increase your speed and the amount of damage should you hit anything!

There are five principal rules to remember:
1. Boats on starboard tack have right of way over those on port tack.
2. Windward boat keeps clear.
3. Overtaking boat keeps clear.
4. Drive on the right.
5. Power gives way to sail.

Starboard tack
The rules define the tack you are on as opposite to the side that the boom is on. Hence, if the boom is over on the port side, you are on the starboard, right-of-way tack. If the boom is on the starboard side, then you are on the port, give-way tack.
It is a good idea to write 'Port' and 'Starboard' on the respective sides of the boom to remind you. If a boat on port tack is approaching on a collision course, shout 'Starboard', just in case they have not seen you. If they continue, be prepared to take avoiding action yourself to prevent a collision.

Wind

Right-of-way boat

Give-way boat

STARBOARD SHOUT

PORT TACK

Right-of-way boat

Give-way boat

Windward boat keeps clear

When two boats approach each other on the same tack, then the windward boat is obliged to keep clear.

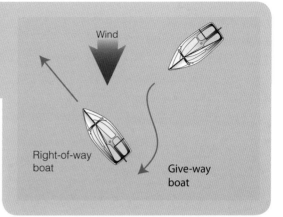

Right-of-way boat

Give-way boat

Wind

Overtaking boat keeps clear

If you are overtaking another boat, sail or power, you must keep clear.

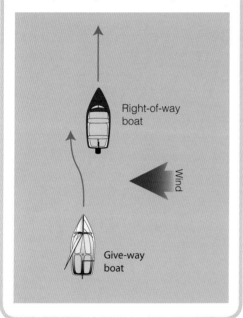

Right-of-way boat

Wind

Give-way boat

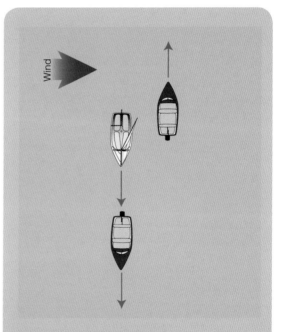

Wind

Power gives way to sail

...but not always. Power is expected to give way to sail in an open seaway, but not in a narrow channel where the manoeuvrability of ships and large vessels is restricted by their draft. This is one where common sense rules and dinghy sailors should never push their luck!

Drive on the right

When sailing in a restricted channel such as a harbour entrance, always stay to the right hand side of the channel. If you intend to cross the channel, then do so at right angles and give way to all vessels travelling up and down the channel.

7. LEAVING AND RETURNING TO SHORE

LEAVING IN AN OFFSHORE WIND

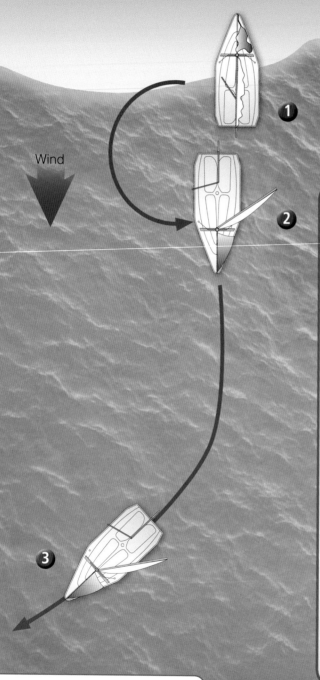

Wind

①

②

③

- Make a last check on wind direction.

- Helm holds bows, allowing crew to step in ready to balance the boat.

- Helm turns bows away from the wind towards the direction you want to sail…

- …pushes off and steps in…

- … pulls rudder downhaul to lock the blade down and steers boat.

- Crew pushes the centreboard down part way.

- Helm and crew set sails to match the wind.

YOU ARE OFF!

LAUNCHING WHEN THE WIND IS ONSHORE

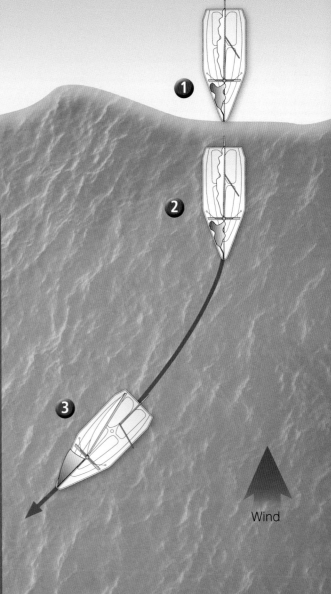

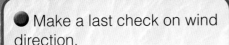

● Make a last check on wind direction.

● Crew holds bows, allowing helm to step in the boat…

● …and pushes the centreboard down part way…

● … then pulls rudder downhaul to lock the blade down and steers boat.

● Crew then pushes the boat off and climbs in.

● Helm and crew set sails to match the wind.

YOU ARE OFF!

Wind

PONTOON LAUNCH WITH AN ONSHORE WIND

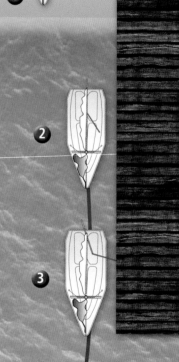

- Make a last check on wind direction.

- Check that bungs are in and transom flaps are shut.

- Hoist sails.

- Launch bow first into the water and hold on to painter (bow rope).

- Tie the boat up.

- Helm climbs aboard, fits the rudder and pulls centreboard part down.

- Crew releases the lines tying boat to pontoon, and walks dinghy to end of pontoon.

- Crew then pushes the boat off and climbs in.

- Helm and crew set sails to match the wind.

Wind

PONTOON LAUNCH WITH AN OFFSHORE WIND

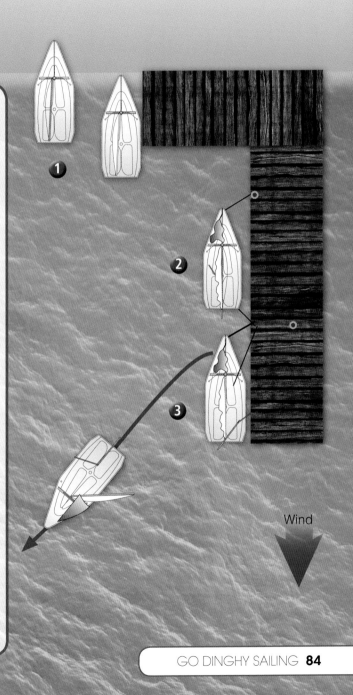

- Make a last check on wind direction.

- Check that bungs are in and transom flaps are shut.

- Launch stern first into the water and hold on to painter (bow rope).

- Tie the boat up to pontoon head to wind.

- Helm climbs aboard, fits the rudder and pulls centreboard part down.

- Helm hoists sails.

- Crew releases the lines tying boat to pontoon, and steps aboard.

- Crew then pushes the boat off, and pulls jib in on pontoon side to turn the bow round.

- Helm pulls tiller hard over to steer boat round.

- Helm and crew set sails to match the wind.

Wind

RETURNING TO SHORE

WINDWARD SHORE

Plan your windward course back to shore and keep the crew fully informed – it is their job to jump out at the right moment and hold the dinghy head to wind.

● On final approach, helm turns boat head to wind and releases rudder tie-down

● Crew pushes up centreboard.

● Crew jumps out when water is shallow enough to hold bow head to wind.

● Helm jumps out, gets trolley, puts it under the boat and with crew, pulls dinghy out of the water.

● Helm and crew work together to lower the sails.

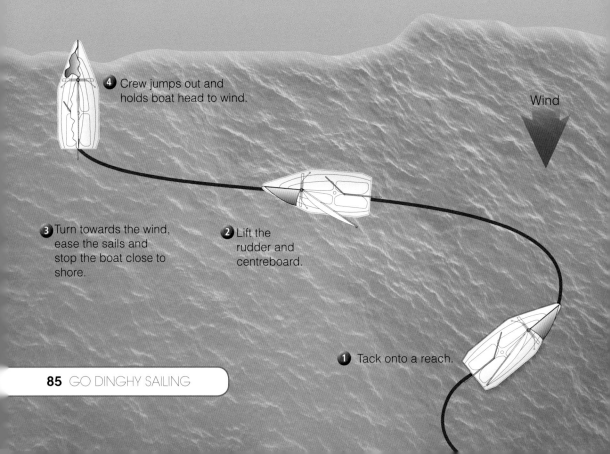

④ Crew jumps out and holds boat head to wind.

Wind

③ Turn towards the wind, ease the sails and stop the boat close to shore.

② Lift the rudder and centreboard.

① Tack onto a reach.

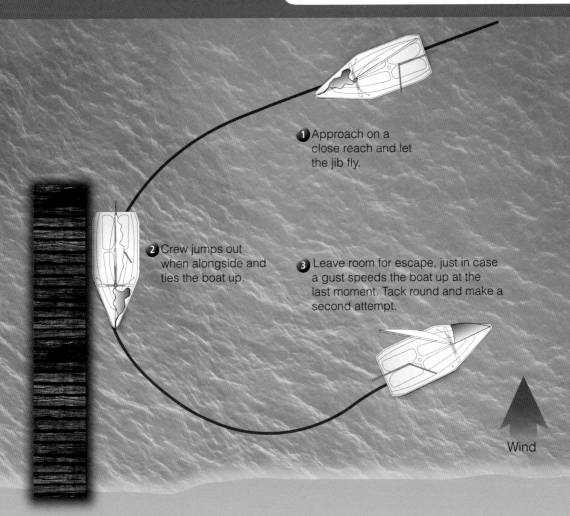

① Approach on a close reach and let the jib fly.

② Crew jumps out when alongside and ties the boat up.

③ Leave room for escape, just in case a gust speeds the boat up at the last moment. Tack round and make a second attempt.

Wind

ALONGSIDE A PONTOON

● As you approach, slow the boat down by letting out the sails and turning head to wind.

● Crew has bow line in hand and prepares to tie boat up to a cleat or jump out to hold the boat once it has stopped. Keep hands clear of the gunwale to avoid them being crushed against the pontoon.

● Once the boat is tied up, helm lowers the sails.

● If you overshoot, tack round and make a second attempt.

RETURNING TO A LEE SHORE

If you are not experienced, avoid beaching on a lee shore. Beginners should only attempt this in calm weather. Should conditions allow:

● Turn head to wind some way off shore, clear of breaking waves and take the mainsail down.

● Turn back downwind, sailing under jib alone.

● Helm releases the rudder downhaul.

● Crew jumps out when water is shallow enough to hold boat steady.

● Helm lowers the jib.

● Helm jumps out, gets the trolley, puts it under the boat and with crew, pulls dinghy out of the water.

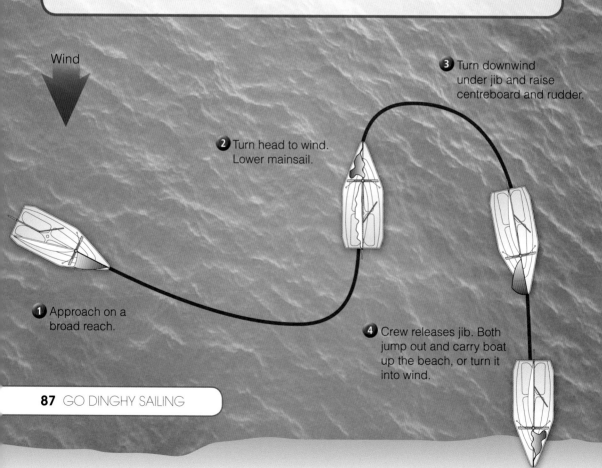

Wind

3 Turn downwind under jib and raise centreboard and rudder.

2 Turn head to wind. Lower mainsail.

1 Approach on a broad reach.

4 Crew releases jib. Both jump out and carry boat up the beach, or turn it into wind.

RETURNING TO A PONTOON BROADSIDE TO THE WIND

● Turn head to wind some way off shore, and take the mainsail down.

● Turn back downwind, sailing under jib alone.

● As helm turns rudder to approach the pontoon, crew releases the jib sheet.

● Crew has painter (bow line) in hand and prepares to tie the boat up to a cleat or jumps out to hold the boat once it has stopped. Keep hands clear of the gunwale to avoid being crushed.

● Once the boat is tied up, helm lowers the jib.

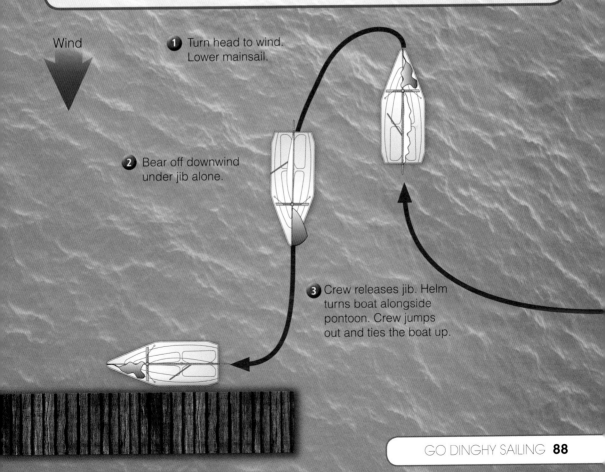

Wind

1 Turn head to wind. Lower mainsail.

2 Bear off downwind under jib alone.

3 Crew releases jib. Helm turns boat alongside pontoon. Crew jumps out and ties the boat up.

8. CAPSIZE AND RECOVERY

CAPSIZE AND RECOVERY

We all capsize at some point, so it is a good idea to practice the recovery routine on a calm day. Children find this great fun, and while some adults may think this is something to avoid, it is not to be feared – the worst that can happen is that you get wet!

Singlehanded recovery

- Swim round or climb over to the weather side and stand on the centreboard.
- Hold on to the gunwale and lean your weight back.
- As the boat comes back upright, it will turn head to wind automatically.

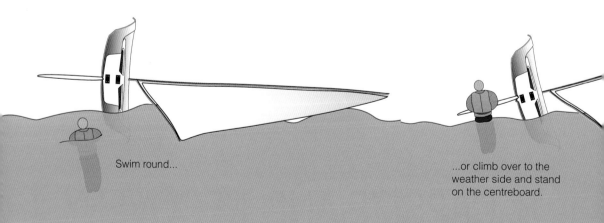

Swim round...

...or climb over to the weather side and stand on the centreboard.

TIP

Don't panic if you become trapped under the sail. Simply push the sail up off the water to create an air pocket and swim out from underneath.

If you become trapped under the boat, take a deep breath and pull yourself out under the gunwale.

⬤ Clamber in over the side.

⬤ Open the bailer or transom flaps.

⬤ Pull in on the mainsheet and resume sailing.

⬤ Never climb in over the stern. Should the sails fill before you are back onboard, the dinghy could take off without you.

Hold on to the gunwale and lean your weight back. As the boat comes back upright, it will turn head to wind automatically.

Scoop method for two-handed recovery

◐ Helm swims round and climbs on the centreboard.

◐ Crew floats facing aft on the opposite side, holding on to the thwart or toe straps.

◐ Helm holds on to the gunwale or sheet, and leans back to pull the boat upright.

◐ As the boat comes back upright, it will turn head to wind automatically and scoop crew up into cockpit.

◐ Helm clambers in over the side.

◐ Helm and crew open the bailers and/or transom flaps.

◐ Helm and crew pull in the sheets and resume sailing.

NEVER CLIMB IN OVER THE STERN. SHOULD THE SAILS FILL BEFORE YOU ARE BACK ONBOARD, THE DINGHY COULD TAKE OFF WITHOUT YOU.

MANOVERBOARD RECOVERY

1 Release the jib

2 Prepare to tack round

MOB

5 Release mainsail to slow the boat down and approach MOB on windward side of the dinghy

If the crew falls overboard, release the jib and prepare to tack round to pick him/her up. If the helm falls out, the crew must first release the jib, then grab the tiller and take charge of the boat.
Above is the routine for returning to the manoverboard position.

GETTING THE MOB BACK ONBOARD

- Kneel on the floor and reach over to grab hold of the person.
- Lean back and pull their body over the gunwale.
- If the MOB is unable to help himself, grab a leg and lift it on board, then roll the victim over the gunwale and into the boat.
- With a catamaran, bring the MOB onboard over either the forward or aft beam.

Wind

WIND

4 Turn up towards the MOB on a close reach

3 Bear off down on a broad reach until 10 boat lengths from MOB

RIGHTING A CATAMARAN

Because of its wider beam and extra windage, a catamaran can often be harder to right than a dinghy, especially if it turns turtle.

⬤ Hold on to the boat at all times.

⬤ Release the sheets and mainsheet traveller to prevent the boat sailing away once it comes back upright.

⬤ Move round to the underside and climb on to the lower hull.

⬤ Grab hold of the righting line or a sheet.

⬤ Turn the boat until the mast is pointing directly into wind in order to use the windage on the trampoline and rig to assist in righting the cat. If necessary, take your weight forward to depress the bow into the water. This will help the cat swing round in the breeze.

⬤ Lean back on the righting line or sheet to lift the mast clear of the water.

⬤ The wind will now help to lift the cat, so be prepared for it to right very quickly.

⬤ Avoid the top hull as it comes over. Try to drop into the water under the forward beam and hold on to it. This will turn the cat up into wind and stop it from sailing off or capsizing again.

⬤ Climb back aboard over one of the beams, sort out all the sheets and start sailing again.

9. BASICS OF WEATHER

SIGNS OF THE WEATHER

Reading the weather is a necessity when sailing. Before setting out, you need to know of predicted changes in the wind, the chance of a gale, and indeed a flat calm, as well as the state of the tides. Local forecasts are readily available on the web and as a phone app, so there is no excuse not to be prepared.

Changes in the weather follow the interaction between four different air masses:

Polar	cold, dry air
Tropical	warm, wet air
Maritime	wet air from non-tropical ocean regions
Continental	dry air from large landmasses

High-Pressure Systems

High-pressure systems (called Highs or anticyclones) bring welcome warm weather and lighter winds. The faster moving low-pressure systems (called Lows or depressions) bring stronger wind conditions.

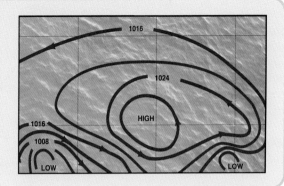

Low-Pressure Systems

These can hold both warm and cold fronts, which are marked on weather maps with a line of triangles (cold fronts) and half circles (warm fronts). A passing front marks a significant change in conditions. A cold front signals cold, dry spells behind; a warm front brings with it warm, wet, tropical air. Expect fast changing conditions with strong, often gusty winds immediately under these fronts, which are heralded by a dramatic change in cloud formation.

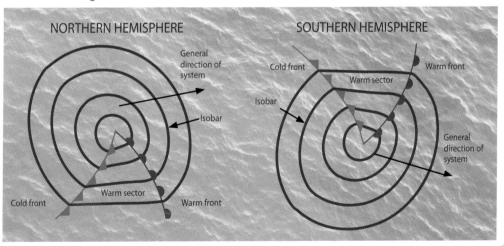

Frontal Systems

High-pressure and low-pressure systems are depicted on weather maps as a series of round or lozenge shaped isobars or lines of equal pressure. Low pressure systems circulate clockwise in the southern hemisphere and anticlockwise in the northern hemisphere. The isobars and the space between them on the map are your first forecasting tool. The closer the lines, the stronger the winds will be.

Local features can also have a significant effect on the winds. Buildings, cliffs and trees will create wind shadows in their lee and produce a funnel effect around them that can catch out the unwary. Inland, the wind can also funnel along river valleys and create conditions that are quite different to the general pattern.

Weather terms	Visibility
Good	More than 5 miles (9kms)
Moderate	2.5–5 miles (4–9kms)
Poor	0.5–2 miles (1–3.5kms)
Fog	Less than 0.5 mile (1km)

● Sea Breeze

In coastal regions, the sea breeze, caused by the temperature difference between land and sea, can produce sparkling sailing conditions at the height of the day when the sun is beating down. In some sunny parts of the world, this convection of air coming in from the sea across the warmer land then rising up to recirculate in the cooler atmosphere, can be so regular that you can set you watch by it. Off Fremantle, Australia, they call this wind 'The Fremantle Doctor' because it calls at the same time each day.

A sea breeze does rely on the upper wind blowing offshore for this circulation to work effectively. If the upper wind is onshore, then this can snuff out the sea breeze altogether, leaving sailors to drift around.

If you are sailing in one area regularly, make a mental note of local peculiarities in the weather so that you can either avoid or take advantage of these micro conditions in the future.

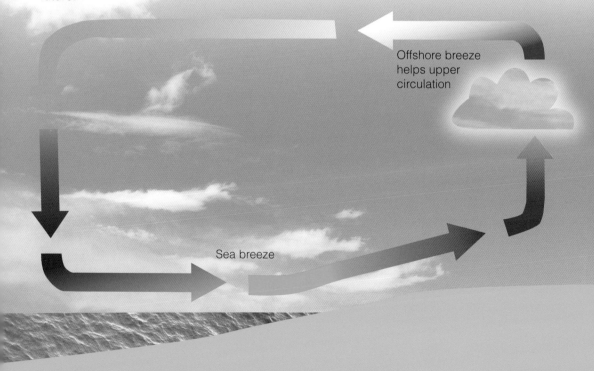

Offshore breeze helps upper circulation

Sea breeze

BEAUFORT WIND SCALE

FORCE	SPEED	DESCRIPTION	OBSERVATIONS
Good beginners' breeze			
0	0–1 knots	Calm	Sea like a mirror. Smoke rises vertically.
1	1–3 knots	Light air	Ripples have appearance of scales on water. Smoke drift and flags indicate direction.
2	4–6 knots	Light breeze	Small wavelets with glassy crests. Wind can be felt on the face. Flags and wind vanes also indicate direction.
3	7–10 knots	Gentle breeze	Large wavelets. Crests begin to break, producing scattered white horses. Leaves and branches begin to move. Ideal conditions to learn to sail. Limit of wind for beginners.
Advanced sailing			
4	11–16 knots	Moderate breeze	Small waves, becoming larger; frequent white horses. Dinghies require more work to keep balanced.
5	17–21 knots	Fresh winds	Moderate waves, take a more pronounced shape with regular white horses formed from spray. Chance of capsize. Small trees sway in wind and flags fly horizontally.
6	22–27 knots	Strong winds	Large waves with white foam crests and spray are extensive. Limit of safety for dinghies. Large trees sway and wind whistles.

10. FIRST STEPS TO RACING

RACING BASICS

Once you have a handle on the basics of sailing, local racing can add a new dimension to your enjoyment and add to your skill level. If you have already bought a dinghy, then join a sailing club that offers racing for your class of boat. If you are not yet sure, then visit your nearest club and offer to crew – you will be welcomed with open arms.

Racing adds a competitive twist to sailing; it is great fun and, 20 years on, you will still be learning new tricks to make your boat go faster and make the best of wind and tides. It is never boring.

Courses vary according to their location. If you are racing on a river, the course has to be laid out within the constraints of the banks and shallows and may lead you around many marks.

As an aide-memoire, it is well worthwhile having a square of self-adhesive plastic stuck down on the deck to mark out the course, as well as wind direction, with a marker pen.

CHECKLIST BEFORE GOING AFLOAT TO RACE

- ☐ Bailer and sponge
- ☐ Battens
- ☐ Buoyancy aid/lifejacket
- ☐ Food and water
- ☐ Protest flag
- ☐ Rudder and tiller
- ☐ Sails
- ☐ Spare shackles and line
- ☐ Timing watch

On open waters, races are set around a traditional triangle, or an upwind/downwind sausage, or a combination of both. Write them down and follow the course exactly (see image right), and avoid passing through the start–finish line if the course line goes outside of these – you could find yourself disqualified otherwise. Details of the course, start times, signals and special rules will be found in sailing instructions published either on a sheet pinned to a notice board along with the course, or on a marker board in the club.

● Starts

Races usually start with an upwind leg with the start line drawn between a committee boat and mark, or a transit line set onshore.

Flags flying from a mast will signal the countdown to the start. Unless the sailing instructions say otherwise, the sequence will start with a flag specific to each class, being flown five minutes before the start, accompanied by a sound signal – usually a gun or horn. When there are multiple starts for different types of boats, there will be a class flag for each, so check which is yours before you set out.

Four minutes from the start, the preparatory Blue Peter flag will be flown accompanied by a second sound signal. At the start, all flags are pulled down and a third sound signal is fired.

If any boats are over the line, a further sound signal is made and the Blue Peter flag will be flown at half mast. It is the duty of those who made a premature start to return and restart, without impeding other boats. Two sound signals signify a general recall for the entire class. The red and white P flag signifies a postponement.

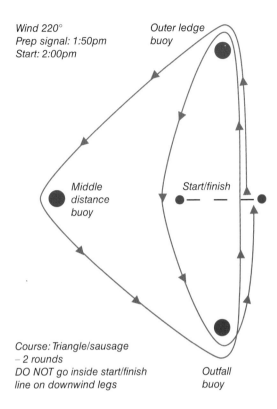

Wind 220°
Prep signal: 1:50pm
Start: 2:00pm

Outer ledge buoy

Middle distance buoy

Start/finish

Course: Triangle/sausage
– 2 rounds
DO NOT go inside start/finish line on downwind legs

Outfall buoy

Blue Peter Preparatory Signal

Postponement Signal

◗ Timed run to the start

The start is all about timing your run to the line and crossing it at full speed clear of other boats moments after the gun has fired. One tried and tested method of hitting the line on cue is the timed run.

Starting from the line, reach off on a reciprocal course to your final close-hauled approach for 1 minute. Allow 15 seconds to tack, and sail close-hauled back to the start line. Wind and tide being equal, you should cross the line exactly 1 minute later. If this works out in practice during the preliminaries before the start, then reach away from the line exactly 2 minutes 15 seconds before the final gun and you should make a great start. If during the practice you find it takes a little longer to turn and sail back, then simply adjust the time you start to reach away from the line accordingly.

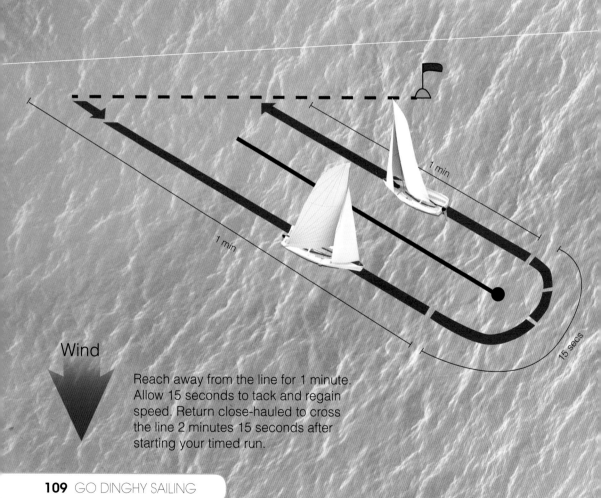

Wind

Reach away from the line for 1 minute. Allow 15 seconds to tack and regain speed. Return close-hauled to cross the line 2 minutes 15 seconds after starting your timed run.

● Around the course

On the beat, try to take advantage of any shifts in the wind, staying on one tack when the winds veer, lifting your heading towards the windward mark, and tacking whenever the wind backs, pushing the boat's heading away from the mark.

Round the marks as closely as possible and set the sails to match the new course as you round them. Try to avoid running dead downwind. It is much more efficient to steer 10–15° either side of the wind, as if on a training run, even if this means gybing to reach the gybe mark.

If you are sailing slower than other boats around you, check to see how they have their sails set and boat trimmed and copy them. Once back on shore, talk to one of the leading crews and ask them for any tuning tips – mast rake and position, sheet fairlead positions etc. They will almost certainly be pleased to continue to give advice – until you start beating them!

11. SAFETY AFLOAT

BASIC SAFETY

Sailing is a great sport that by-and-large is also safe. It certainly is for those who treat wind and water with respect, wear buoyancy aids or lifejackets as a matter of course, carry appropriate safety equipment and know how to summon help if it is needed.

● Safety equipment to have in a dinghy

INLAND WATERS
Buoyancy aids
Paddle
Bailer

COASTAL WATERS
Buoyancy aids or
life-jackets
Paddle
Bailer
Folding anchor and line
Tow line

Knife
Waterproof bag
Mobile phone
Energy drinks
Energy bars

CRUISING IN COASTAL WATERS
Buoyancy aids or life jackets
Coastal flare pack
Basic first-aid kit
Paddle

Bailer
Folding anchor and line
Tow line
Knife
Waterproof charts
Compass
Waterproof bag
Mobile phone
Energy drinks
Energy bars

● How to summon assistance

If you get into difficulties, can't cope and need assistance, you can summon other boats around you by raising and lowering your arms or firing off a flare.
The quickest way to alert the emergency services is to dial 999 on your mobile phone.
Alternatively, firing flares will alert passers-by to call the Coastguard for you.

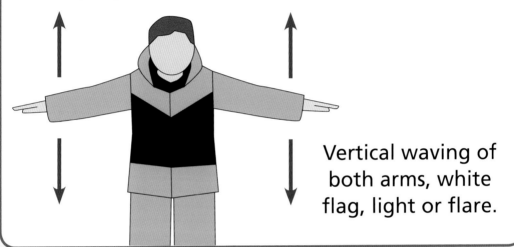

Vertical waving of both arms, white flag, light or flare.

GLOSSARY OF TERMS

ABACK – When the jib is sheeted to the windward side and the dinghy is hove-to.

ABAFT – Behind or towards the stern.

ABEAM – At right angles to the boat.

AFT – See Abaft.

AIRFLOW – Flow of air across the sails.

AMIDSHIPS – Centre of the boat.

ABOUT – To go about is to tack the dinghy through the wind.

ANCHOR – Portable device to moor the dinghy in open water on the end of a line.

ANEMOMETER – Instrument to measure wind speed.

ANTICYCLONE – Meteorological term describing area of high pressure.

APPARENT WIND – The wind experienced by a moving boat. If the boat is stationary, the apparent wind is the same as the true wind. If the boat is moving towards the wind, the apparent wind is greater than the true wind. If the boat is moving away from the wind, the apparent wind is less than the true wind.

ASYMMETRIC SPINNAKER – Downwind sail with a fixed luff, which is tacked or gybed like a jib.

BACKING THE JIB – Setting the jib on the weather side to encourage the boat to bear away.

BACKWIND – When the airflow across the jib causes the mainsail to flutter.

BAILER – Scoop to remove water from inside the boat.

BATTEN – Flexible strip of wood or reinforced resin to stiffen the leech of the sail.

BEAM – Mid part of the dinghy, or measurement of maximum width of the hull.

BEAM REACH – Sailing with the wind directly abeam.

BEAR AWAY – To turn the bows away from the wind.

BEARING – Compass direction.

BEAT – The close-hauled, zigzag course to windward.

BEATING – Sailing close-hauled to windward.

BEAUFORT SCALE – Scale of wind speeds devised by Admiral Sir Francis Beaufort.

BERMUDA RIG – Single masted sail plan with tall, triangular mainsail.

BIGHT – An open loop in a rope.

BLACK BANDS – Narrow bands painted on the mast and boom to mark the maximum extension of the mainsail luff and foot.

BLOCK – A pulley.

BLOCK AND TACKLE – A multi-purchase pulley system.

BOLT ROPE – Rope sewn or enclosed in the luff of the mainsail.

BOOM – Spar attached to the foot of the mainsail – and sometimes the jib.

BOOM VANG – Multi-purchase system or lever, also known as a kicking strap, to prevent the boom from rising and to control the shape of the mainsail.

BOTTLE SCREW – Screw system used to tension rigging.

BOW – Front end of the dinghy.

BOWLINE – A knot used to tie a loop into the end of a rope.

BOWSPRIT – Spar that extends forward of the bow to support an asymmetric spinnaker on a dinghy.

BREAKWATER – Small upstanding ledge or coaming across the foredeck to deflect water.

BROACH – When a dinghy slews out of control broadside to the wind and sea.

BROAD REACH – Point of sail when wind is abaft the beam.

BULKHEAD – Transverse partition within the boat.

BUNG – Plug to block a drainage hole.

BUOY – Floating racing mark or navigation mark.

BUOYANCY – Power to float, having a density less than water.

BUOYANCY BAGS/TANKS – Built-in buoyancy to support the dinghy in the event of a capsize.

BURGEE – Small flag flown from the masthead.

 C

CAM CLEAT – Cleat with two spring-load cams to hold a rope.

CAMBER – Curvature of a sail.

CAPSIZE – Point when the mast of a dinghy touches the water.

CATAMARAN – Twin-hulled vessel.

CENTRE OF BUOYANCY – Point where the buoyant force of water acts on the hull.

CENTRE OF EFFORT – Point where the force of wind acts on the rig.

CENTRE OF PRESSURE – Point where the side force of wind acts on the hull.

CENTREBOARD – Retractable keel that limits leeway, or the sideways force of the sails.

CHAIN PLATE – Hull or deck fitting to which the shroud is attached.

CHART – Map of the sea.

CHINE – Line or crease in the hull. A dinghy built from flat sheets of plywood is known as a hard chine boat.

CHINESE GYBE – Involuntary crash gybe.

CLEAT – Fitting designed to hold a rope under tension without the use of a knot or hitch.

CLEW – Lower, aft corner of a sail.

CLEW OUTHAUL – Adjustor to change tension on the clew, and shape of the sail.

CLINKER CONSTRUCTION – Traditional form of hull construction where the planks overlap each other.

CLOSE REACH – Point of sailing midway between close-hauled and a beam reach.

CLOSE–HAULED – Point of sailing closest to wind.

CLOVE HITCH – Common knot or hitch used to tie a rope to a ring or rail.

COAMING – Small upstanding ledge or breakwater across or around the deck to deflect water.

COCKPIT – Area of the dinghy where helm and crew operate the boat.

COMPASS – Navigation instrument that points to the magnetic north pole.

CRINGLE – Metal eye or attachment point in each corner of the sail.

CUNNINGHAM HOLE – Cringle in luff to attach a purchase to flatten the sail.

CURRENT – A stream of water.

 D

DACRON – American name for man-made sail material named polyester in Europe.

DAGGERBOARD – A vertically retracting keel that limits leeway, or the sideways force of the sails.

DEAD RUN – Sailing dead downwind.

DEPRESSION – Meteorological term for an area of low pressure.

DEVIATION – Compass error influenced by magnetic materials nearby.

DINGHY – Small open boat without a fixed keel.

DIRTY WIND – Disturbed wind or wind shadow effect from a dinghy to windward.

DISPLACEMENT – Volume/weight that a hull displaces in water.

DOWNHAUL – Rope or purchase used to tension the tack of a sail or Cunningham.

DOWNWIND – Sailing in the same direction as the wind.

 E

EASE – To slacken a rope or let a sheet out.

EBB – Outgoing tide or flow.

EDDIES – Area of reverse or back-running current.

 F

FAIRLEAD – A fixed lead to guide a rope or sheet and prevent chafe.

FAIRWAY – Main navigable channel.

FAIR WIND – Wind direction that allows a boat to sail from A to B without tacking.

FATHOM – Nautical unit of measure equal to 6ft (1.828m).

FENDER – Portable cushion or inflatable bladder to protect the hull from rubbing against another boat or a pontoon.

FETCH – Straight course sailed to windward without tacking.

FIGURE-OF-EIGHT KNOT – Stopper knot.

FOILS – Collective term for keel, centreboard/ daggerboard and rudder.

FLOOD TIDE – A rising tide.

FOLLOWING WIND – Opposite of headwind, when the wind comes from astern.

FORESAIL – Jib.

FORESTAY – Forward stay supporting the mast.

FREEBOARD – Height of a boat's side above the water.

FRONT – Meteorological term describing a distinct line of weather – cold front, warm front etc.

FURL – To gather up or reef a sail in an orderly manner.

 G

GAFF – Spar supporting the top of a traditional four-sided mainsail – gaff rig.

GATE START – Method of starting a race with fleet passing behind the stern of a guard boat tracking behind a dinghy sailing close-hauled on port tack.

GEL COAT – The smooth waterproof outer resin coating of a fibre-reinforced moulded hull and deck.

GENOA – Large headsail that overlaps the mainsail.

GNAV – Upward facing version of a vang or kicking strap used to prevent the boom from rising and control the shape of the mainsail.

GO ABOUT – To tack through the eye of the wind.

GOOSENECK – Double-hinged fitting to attach boom to mast.

GOOSE-WINGED – Running before the wind with mainsail set on one side and jib 'goose-winged' out on the other.

GPS – Satellite-based global positioning system.

GRADIENT WIND – Meteorological term caused by changes in barometric pressure. The greater the change in pressure, the steeper the gradient.

GRP – Glass reinforced plastic.

GUDGEON – Female part of a pair of rudder hangings into which the male pintle fits.

GUNTER RIG – Traditional high-aspect mainsail with gaff that extends almost vertically up from the mast.

GUNWALE – Outer strengthening piece around the top of the hull.

GUY – Windward spinnaker sheet or boom restrainer.

GYBE – Controlled form of tacking downwind when the transom passes through the eye of the wind and the boom flies across from one side to the other.

HALF HITCH – Temporary knot to attach a rope to a rail.

HALYARD – Rope or wire line to hoist sails up the mast.

HANK – Clip to attach luff or sail to a stay.

HARD CHINE – Line where the flat sheets used to construct a hull meet.

HARDEN UP – To point closer to wind.

HEAD – Top corner of a sail.

HEADBOARD – Reinforced top corner of a mainsail.

HEADING – Direction that a boat is taking.

HEADSAIL – Jib or genoa.

HEADSTAY – Forward stay supporting the mast.

HEAD TO WIND – Boat facing directly into wind - the no-go zone...

HEAVE TO – To bring the boat to a halt, head to wind, by backing the jib, putting the rudder down and letting the mainsail fly.

HEEL – Bottom end of the mast. The sideways tilt of a sailing boat.

HELM – Rudder. Also short for helmsman or helmsperson.

HIGHFIELD LEVER – A locking lever to tension stays.

HIKE – To sit out and counter the heeling force of the wind.

HITCH – Type of knot for attaching a rope to a rail or hoop.

HOIST – Vertical dimension of a sail or flag.

HOUNDS – Where the shrouds connect to the mast.

HOVE TO – See Heave to.

IMMINENT – Meteorological term for change in weather within six hours.

INGLEFIELD CLIPS – Interlocking C-shaped clips used to attach signal flaps, and sometimes a spinnaker, to a halyard.

IN IRONS – Term used when a sailboat is caught head to wind within the no-go zone.

ISOBAR – Meteorological term for line on weather map linking points of equal atmospheric pressure.

JIB – headsail.

JIB SHEETS – Ropes controlling the set of the jib.

JIB STICK – Pole to goose-wing the jib from when sailing dead downwind. Also known as a whisker pole.

JUMPER STAY – Stay on the foreside of the mast to limit the amount of bend in the spar.

KICKING STRAP – Multi-purchase system or lever, also known as a vang, to prevent the boom from rising and control the shape of the mainsail.

KITE – Abbreviation for spinnaker.

KNOT – Nautical mile per hour (1 nautical mile equals 1.15 statute miles or 1,852m). Also refers to a rope tie.

KNUCKLE – Sharp longitudinal line of distortion within the hull.

LAND BREEZE – Offshore wind opposite to a sea breeze, that develops when the temperature of the sea is higher than the land.

LANYARD – Short length of cord used as a safety line.

LATERAL RESISTANCE – Ability of a boat to resist leeway or sideways force of the wind.

LEAD – The direction that a rope is led.

LEE – Opposite to windward. The side away from the wind.

LEECH – Trailing edge of a sail.

LEE BOW – Sailing on a tack where the tidal stream carries the boat towards the wind.

LEE HELM – A sailing boat, which requires its tiller to be pushed down to the leeward side to counter the boat's natural tendency to bear away, is said to carry 'lee helm'. This condition signifies that the rig is out of balance with the hull.

LEE HO – Final warning call of helm as the tiller is pushed over to leeward during a tack.

LEE SHORE – Shoreline which the wind is blowing towards.

LEEWARD – Opposite of windward; away from the wind.

LIFEJACKET – Buoyancy vest designed to keep a non-swimmer or unconscious person floating head up.

LIFT – A shift in the wind that swings aft. Otherwise known as a freeing wind.

LOA – Length overall.

LOOSE-FOOTED – Sail attached to a boom only by the clew and outhaul.

LUFF – The leading edge of a sail.

LUFFING – When a sailboat is steered closer to the wind.

LUFF ROPE – Rope sewn or enclosed in the luff of the mainsail. Also known as boltrope.

LWL – Load waterline or length of waterline.

M

MAGNETIC NORTH – Compass heading.

MAGNETIC VARIATION – Difference in angle between true north and magnetic north.

MAINSAIL – Principal sail set on a mast.

MAINSHEET – Rope attached to the boom to trim the mainsail.

MARLING HITCH – Line of linked knots tying sail to a spar.

MILLIBAR – Meteorological term for unit of pressure equal to 1/10000th of a bar.

MOULD – Male or female pattern for producing a plastic hull and other mouldings.

MULTIHULL – Generic term for a catamaran or trimaran.

N

NAUTICAL MILE – 1 nautical mile equals 1.15 statute miles or 1,852m.

NEAP TIDES – Tides with the smallest rise and fall. Opposite of spring tides.

NO-GO ZONE – Area 40° either side of the direction of the wind.

O

OFFSHORE WIND – Wind blowing seaward off the land.

OFFWIND – Sailing in the same direction as the wind.

OFF THE WIND – Sailing a course lower than a beam reach.

ONSHORE WIND – Wind blowing inland off the sea.

ON THE WIND – Sailing a close-hauled course.

OUTHAUL – Line used to stretch the clew of a sail to the end of the boom.

P

PAINTER – Mooring line.

PELICAN HOOK – Metal hook with a cam-action lock.

PFD – Personal flotation device such as a buoyancy aid or lifejacket.

PINCH – Sailing so close to the wind that the sails start to luff and lose drive.

PINTLE – Male part of a pair of rudder hangings that fits into the female gudgeon.

PITCHPOLE – When a boat capsizes end over end.

PLANING – When a boat lifts its bows out of the water, and because of the reduced drag, then accelerates onto to a planing attitude.

POLED OUT – Running before the wind with mainsail set on one side and the jib poled out or 'goose-winged' on the other.

POINTS OF SAILING – Beating, reaching and running before the wind.

PORT – Left-hand side of a boat.

PORT GYBE – Sailing downwind with the wind on the port side of the boat and mainsail out to port. This is the give-way gybe.

PORT TACK – Sailing with the wind on the port (left) side of the boat. This is the give-way tack.

PORTSMOUTH YARDSTICK – Simple dinghy handicapping system when mixed classes race together.

PRE-BEND – Amount of fore and aft bend set in a mast.

PREVENTER – Safety line.

PURCHASE – Mechanical advantage of the block and tackle or lever.

Q

QUARTER – Sides of the boat aft, i.e. starboard quarter, port quarter.

R

RACE – Fast running tide or stream.

RACING FLAG/PENNANT – Small rectangular flag flown at the masthead to signal that the boat is racing.

RAKE – Degree that a mast leans back from vertical.

RATCHET BLOCK – Purchase block with an integral ratchet to lessen the load of a sheet held in the hand.

REACH – Sailing course with the wind abeam.

REACHING – Sailing with the wind abeam.

REACHING HOOK – Device set close to the shrouds to run the windward spinnaker sheet or guy through.

READY ABOUT – First warning call to the crew that the helm intends to tack.

REEF – To reduce or shorten sail.

REEF KNOT – Knot joining two ropes together.

RIDING TURN – When a rope or sheet crosses under itself and jams, most often around a winch.

RIG – General term for mast, spars and sails.

RIGGING – Standing wires that hold up the mast.

RIGGING SCREW – Screw to tension shrouds. Also known as a bottle screw.

RIGHT OF WAY – Term within Collision Regulations denoting a boat with rights, as opposed to a boat that must give way.

ROACH – The top curve within the leech of a mainsail.

ROCKER – Fore and aft curve within the central underside sections of the boat.

ROLL TACKING – Use of crew weight to speed the process of tacking to windward.

ROLLER JIB – Furling headsail.

ROTATING MAST – Spar designed to rotate from port to starboard to present its best aspect to the wind.

ROUND TURN AND TWO HALF HITCHES – Knot used to attach rope to a rail or hoop.

RUBBING STRAKE – A strengthening strip secured to the gunwale as a protective buffer.

RUDDER – Moving foil to steer the boat with.

RUN – Sailing dead downwind.

RUNNING BY THE LEE – Sailing downwind with the mainsail set on the windward side and about to gybe.

RUNNING RIGGING – Sheets and halyards used to set and control the sails.

S

SEA BREEZE –– Onshore wind opposite to a land breeze, that develops when the temperature of the land is higher than the sea.

SELF BAILER – Thru-hull bailer that, once activated, allows the bilge water to flow out when the dinghy is planing.

SHACKLE – Metal link with screw pin to connect wires and lines.

SHEAVE – The wheel within a block.

SHEET – Any rope used to adjust sail shape.

SHEET BEND – Knot used to join two dissimilar sized ropes together.

SHOCK CORD – Elastic or bungee cord made of rubber strands.

SHROUDS – Wires supporting either side of the mast.

SLAB REEF – Method of reefing the mainsail.

SLIP LINE – Temporary double line with both ends made fast to the boat that can be released from onboard and pulled in.

SLOT EFFECT – The effect a jib has in accelerating the flow of air around the back of a mainsail.

SNAP SHACKLE – Shackle with a secure locking mechanism instead of a pin.

SPAR – General term for a mast, boom, gaff or spinnaker pole.

SPINNAKER – Large parachute-like downwind sail.

SPINNAKER CHUTE – Open-mouthed tubular container fitted in the bow of a dinghy from which to launch and recover the spinnaker.

SPINNAKER POLE – Spar to set the spinnaker from.

SPREADER – A strut usually fitted in pairs to deflect the shrouds and control the bending characteristics of the mast.

SPRING TIDE – Extreme high tide caused by the gravitational pull of the moon.

SQUALL – Sudden, short-lived increase in wind.

STAND ON BOAT – Right-of-way boat.

STARBOARD – Right-hand side of the boat.

STARBOARD GYBE – Sailing downwind with the wind on the starboard side of the boat and mainsail out to port. This is the right-of-way gybe.

STARBOARD TACK – Sailing upwind with the wind on the starboard side of the boat and mainsail out to port. This is the right-of-way tack.

STAY – Forward mast support.

STEM – Forward extremity of the boat.

STERN – Aft extremity of the boat.

STOPPER – A cleating device that holds a sheet or halyard fast.

STROP – A ring of rope or wire used to make up an attachment to a spar.

SWIVEL – Connector whose two parts rotate.

SWIVEL BLOCK – Block with a swivel joint.

TABERNACLE – Structure supporting a deck-stepped mast.

TACK – Lower forward corner of a sail.

TACKING – To sail close-hauled through the eye of the wind.

TACKLE – Multi-purchase system.

TAIL – The free end of a sheet or halyard.

TALURIT – Swaged wire splice.

TELLTALES – Strips of fabric or wool attached to the luff of a jib and leech of the mainsail to indicate airflow across the sail.

TIDE – Six-hourly rise and fall of water caused by the gravitational pull of the moon.

TILLER – Arm of a rudder to control boat direction.

TILLER EXTENSION – Lightweight pole with universal joint attached to the end of the tiller to allow the helm to sit outboard or steer from the trapeze.

TOE STRAPS – Lengths of webbing running fore and aft in a dinghy for crew to hook their feet under and hike out.

TRAILING EDGE – Aft edge of a foil, i.e. sail, keel, rudder etc.

TRAINING RUN – Sailing downwind 5-10° shy of the dead downwind angle.

TRAMPOLINE – Rope netting or webbing strung between two hulls of a catamaran.

TRANSIT – Sighting two objects in line.

TRANSOM – Transverse aft end of a boat.

TRANSOM FLAP – Flaps that open at the stern to allow water to escape from a planing dinghy following a capsize.

TRAPEZE – Harness attached by wire to the hounds of the mast to allow the crew to extend their whole body outboard of the dinghy to improve their righting moment.

TRAVELLER – Fitting on a rope or track with limited travel used to adjust the mainsheet.

TRIM – To adjust the sails to suit the wind direction.

TRIMARAN – Three-hulled multihull.

TRUE WIND – Direction and velocity of wind measured at a stationary position.

TWIST – Difference in angle to the wind between the top and bottom of a sail.

UNIVERSAL JOINT – Hinge that allows universal movement.

UNSTAYED MAST – Mast without standing rigging.

UPHAUL – Control line to adjust the height of the spinnaker pole.

UPWIND – Any course closer to the wind than a beam reach.

VANG – Multi-purchase system or lever, also known as a kicking strap, to prevent the boom from rising and control the shape of the mainsail.

VARIATION – Difference in angle between true north and magnetic north.

VMG – Velocity made good to windward.

WAKE – Turbulence left astern of a moving boat.

WARP – Rope used to moor a boat.

WEATHER HELM – A sailing boat, which requires its tiller to be held up towards the weather side to counter the boat's natural tendency to luff, is said to carry 'weather helm'. This condition signifies that the rig is out of balance with the hull.

WEATHER SHORE – Shoreline where the wind is blowing offshore.

WETTED SURFACE – Total underwater area of the hull.

WHISKER POLE – Pole to goose-wing the jib from when sailing dead downwind. Also known as a jib stick.

WINCH – Capstan used to tension sail sheets and halyards.

WINDAGE – Drag caused by the boat and crew.

WINDLASS – See Winch.

WINDWARD – Towards the wind; opposite of leeward.

WIND GRADIENT – Difference in wind speed close to the water and a certain height above it such as the masthead. This is not the same as gradient wind, which refers to changes in barometric pressure.

WORKING END – End of a rope used to tie a knot.

INDEX

ACKNOWLEDGEMENTS

Our thanks go to Hannah Leech at Adlard Coles for her invaluable advice and support during the production of this book and to David Robinson and staff at the UKSA who gamefully acted as our models.

My appreciation also goes to Laser Performance, RS Sailing, and Topper International for generously supplying information and photographs.

I am also indebted to PPL's team of designers, Kayleigh Reynolds, Greg Filip and George Gray and to Andrew Wetherall and his picture research team at PPL Photo Agency for sourcing the many images we needed to illustrate particular points.

Design and illustrations: Kayleigh Reynolds, Greg Filip and George Gray.

Photo research: PPL Photo Agency.

Photography:
Peter Bentley/PPL: 13 David Freeman/PPL: 104 Nick Kirk/PPL: 16 Barry Pickthall/PPL: 17, 46, 47, 48, 49, 50, 51, 93, 94, 97/98, 111/112, 113 Laser Performance: 4/5, 14, 18, 19/20 RS Sailing: ii/iii, 1, 5, 6, 7, 9, 16, 17, 21/22, 30, 36, 43/44, 45, 46, 54, 55/56, 60, 69, 79/80, 89/90, 99/100, 105/106, 107, 110, 113, 114, 121
Topper International: iv/v, 15, 18, 51, 52, 87, 91, 92, 97